Foreign Direct Investment in Latin America

Manuel R. Agosin
Editor

Published by the Inter-American Development Bank
Distributed by The Johns Hopkins University Press

Washington, D.C.
1995

The views and opinions expressed in this publication are those of the authors and do not necessarily reflect the official position of the Inter-American Development Bank.

Foreign Direct Investment in Latin America

© Copyright 1995 by the Inter-American Development Bank
JK

Inter-American Development Bank
1300 New York Avenue, N.W.
Washington, D.C. 20577

Distributed by
The Johns Hopkins University Press
2715 North Charles Street
Baltimore, MD 21218-4319

Library of Congress Catalog Card Number: 95-81780
ISBN: 1-886938-01-6

AUTHORS

Agosin, Manuel R.
Director of Graduate Studies in Economics and Administration, and Director, Economics Department, University of Chile, Santiago.

Chudnovsky, Daniel
Researcher, Centro de Investigaciones para la Transformación (CENIT), Buenos Aires, Argentina.

Giedion, Ursula
Researcher, FEDESARROLLO, Bogotá, Colombia.

López, Andrés
Researcher, CENIT, Buenos Aires, Argentina.

Porta, Fernando
Researcher, CENIT, Buenos Aires, Argentina.

Riveros, Luis
Dean, Faculty of Economic and Administrative Sciences, and Professor, Department of Economics, Santiago, Chile.

Steiner, Roberto
Researcher, FEDESARROLLO, Bogotá, Colombia.

Vatter, Jaime
Professor, Department of Economics, University of Chile, Santiago.

FOREWORD

The concept of foreign direct investment (FDI) held by both academics as well as economic policymakers has recently undergone a major change. At present, there is a general consensus that foreign direct investment can make substantial contributions to national development. These contributions include the coinvestment made by national agents, the opening of new marketing channels for local products on international markets, the introduction of new products, technologies and management techniques, and human resource training. Nevertheless, there is less clarity as to which foreign investment policies can maximize these benefits. This book looks at these topics.

Since the late 1980s, FDI into Latin American countries has shown a sharp increase, and, during the 1990s, the countries of the region have been major magnets for these capital flows. For their part, most Latin American countries have significantly liberalized their FDI regimens as part of the shift in their economic policies that give the market the main role in resource allocation. Nevertheless, FDI flows have been concentrated in only a few countries.

In view of the significance of these recent FDI flows and the hopes placed in them by the countries of the region, the Network of Centers for Applied Economic Research included FDI as one of its research projects for the third round. It is hoped that this project will reply to a series of questions on economic policy as it relates to FDI. Is liberalization of the treatment of transnational enterprises sufficient for a country to attract greater flows of FDI? What other policies are required to achieve this objective? Has the recent wave of FDI contributed to the development of the region? What lessons has it left to the countries of the region in terms of policies that seek to maximize the contribution of FDI to development? What has been the role of debt capitalization and privatization programs in attracting and channeling foreign investment towards sectors and activities that can maximize the contributions of FDI to development?

In an attempt to reply to these questions, within the context of this project three national studies (for Argentina, Chile and Colombia) were carried out, each of which is the subject of a chapter of this book. The introductory chapter contains the results of these national studies, and at the same time represents a regional study in itself. A novel aspect of the project is that it addressed the reasons for investment decisions by enterprises and the impact of recent investments on development by means of a survey among the managerial personnel of enterprises with recent investments.

The research yielded certain interesting conclusions with respect to a number of concerns held by the countries in relation to their foreign investment policies. These include the role that should be played by the foreign investment liberalization regimen; incentives and performance requirements; complementary policies in the areas of macroeconomics, taxation, foreign exchange and trade; and foreign debt conversion programs.

Nohra Rey de Marulanda, Manager
Integration and Regional Programs Department

CONTENTS

F21, 016

CHAPTER ONE

FOREIGN DIRECT INVESTMENT IN LATIN AMERICA

Manuel R. Agosin*

Since the late 1980s, the inflow of foreign direct investment (FDI) into the countries of Latin America has surged tremendously. Within a broader context, this phenomenon is part of the overall return of foreign capital following the extended capital "drought" associated with the region's debt crisis.[1] This study evaluates the volume of these new FDI inflows, the factors that have attracted them to the region, and their contribution to Latin American development. This research has utilized studies of three specific Latin American countries (Argentina, Chile and Colombia), as well as additional regionwide data.

This chapter consists of five sections. The first examines the increase of FDI to the region. This increase, although sizable, has thus far been concentrated in just a few countries (Argentina, Chile, Colombia, Mexico and Venezuela). In addition, a good part of the FDI inflow has occurred in response to recent privatization or debt capitalization processes. The relative importance of these processes and their impact on FDI will be analyzed in some detail.

The second section describes the changes that have occurred in the region's foreign investment legislation in recent years, situating these changes within the wider context of general reforms that have tended to grant the market itself a growing role in the region's economies. Most Latin American countries have significantly liberalized their regulations on FDI, to such a degree that the countries no longer seek simply to regulate the transnational enterprises (TEs) that

---

* The editor gratefully acknowledges the comments and suggestions of Ricardo Bielchowski, Alvaro Calderón, Ricardo Ffrench-Davis, Jorge Katz, Alberto Melo, Michael Mortimore, Eduardo Mogano, José Antonio Ocampo, John Page, Guillermo Rosenwurcel, Jorge Sapoznikow, and Alejandro Vera. The Joint ECLAC-UNCTAD Unit on Transnational Enterprises provided valuable statistical and legal information. The efficient research assistance of Christian Fresard is also gratefully acknowledged.
[1] For a detailed discussion, see Ocampo (1994).

wish to set up operations within their borders. In fact, the countries actively compete among themselves for such TE investments.

The third section analyzes the causes of the recent FDI increase in the region. The case studies are based on a sample surveying the transnational enterprises operating in the respective countries, and also on more conventional analytical methods such as econometric studies. These case studies and other recent research indicate that the following factors (in order of importance) have been pivotal in attracting direct investment to the region:

- Special incentives or systems for enterprises in selected economic sectors or for foreign investment in particular.
- Macroeconomic and political stability, as well as stability in the rules governing transnational enterprises.
- Attractive Latin American domestic markets.
- The improved outlook for regional integration.
- The possibility of exporting to developed country markets.

In no case except that of Mexico did the TEs' decisions or future plans seem to have been significantly swayed by the possibility of the host country's eventually signing a free trade agreement with the United States. Nor did the world recession and the decrease in the relative profitability levels in the TEs' major markets significantly influence the TEs' decisions.

In part, the recent FDI surge also corresponds to a simple correction of FDI volumes up from the low levels experienced during the debt crisis, thanks in part to the successful handling of the crisis, the achievement of greater macroeconomic stability in the major FDI recipient countries, and the special privatization and debt capitalization programs such as those implemented by Argentina, Chile and Mexico.

The fourth section discusses the contribution of recent FDI flows to regional development. Three variables figure strongly in this context: the FDI's contribution to capital formation, its contribution to export expansion and diversification (as proxies for international competitiveness), and the FDI's advancement of technological innovation (including the introduction of new products and production processes and new management techniques, and the enhancement of workers' skills through specific training).

The conclusions discussed in this section are based primarily on the national surveys carried out in Argentina, Chile and Colombia. The study on Chile also includes econometric estimates that attempt to quantify the contribution of foreign investment to capital formation. The contribution of FDI to development has been important not only in Chile but also in Argentina and Mexico, where TEs have actually led the capital formation process. Only in Chile, however, has there been a sustained increase in the investment coefficient, indicating that in the other countries, investment from national sources has been weak. In Colombia, in particular, foreign direct investment has been much more modest and therefore its contribution to raising overall investment rates relatively small.

One of the more interesting survey results is that the frequent distinction between the purchase of existing assets versus greenfield investments is actually of relatively small significance in economic terms. In most instances when a foreign investor entered the host country's market through the purchase of domestic enterprises (whether wholly or through joint ventures), the initial purchase of assets ended up being only a small portion of the total investment.

In most Latin American countries that have experienced significant new FDI inflows, the investments do not appear to have made any key contribution to the host countries' export position in the world economy. One exception has been Mexico, where the primary motivation of TEs has been to benefit from Mexico's integration into the North American market. Furthermore, in Mexico, FDI has focused largely upon the manufacturing sector (Huss, 1992; Casar 1993).

Chile has also been an exception, in a sense. FDI in Chile has indeed focused largely on export activities (and also services), but half of that investment has been directed toward large-scale copper mining, a traditional Chilean export sector. In recent years, stimulated by Chile's debt conversion program, FDI has also been strongly attracted to Chile's lumber, paper and cellulose industries—relatively new export sectors, but nonetheless linked to Chile's traditional comparative advantage. With respect to Argentina and Colombia, export diversification has not been a major thrust of the new FDI inflows. In Argentina, the creation of MERCOSUR and the prospects of an expanded regional market have attracted several important investments. In Colombia, the foreign entrepreneurs attracted by that country's domestic market have also cited the prospects for regional integration with Venezuela and within the Andean Pact as incentives for future investments.

In Mexico there is evidence that important technological contributions have indeed been made by foreign investors. But of the three countries examined in this study, FDI's technological contribution has been significant only in Argentina, particularly in the privatized public services sector, where foreign investors were required to make such technological improvements as plant modernization, service improvements, introduction of new management techniques, and labor training. Argentina's industrial sector has also introduced state-of-the-art technology via the new FDI inflows, as in the Argentine automotive industry, where labor productivity has increased considerably. The technological contribution by FDI has been less pronounced in Chile and Colombia, perhaps because technological improvements did not constitute, in those cases, an explicit objective in the negotiations with the foreign entrepreneurs. Another reason is because a large portion of FDI in Chile and Colombia has been directed toward natural resource extraction or processing activities for which there are only slim possibilities of transferring genuinely new technologies.

The fifth and final section of this chapter puts forth various policy recommendations. First, it is clear that in order to attract bigger and better FDI inflows, it will not suffice merely to liberalize FDI legislation. Liberalization of legislation should form part of a cohesive economic development strategy that is both stable and well implemented. The adoption of liberal policies is a necessary but insufficient condition for attracting a sizable inflow of FDI that will strengthen the host country's developmental capacity. Of equal or even greater importance is ensuring stability of the rules of the game (not only for FDI but also for macroeconomic, tax and trade policies). In addition, the existence of special systems that attract foreign investment in priority development sectors has been fundamental in two of the three countries for which national studies are available.

Second, skillful management of the potential host country's debt conversion programs can help increase FDI inflows and direct them toward priority sectors. While debt conversion programs cannot be expected singlehandedly to induce the desired inflows of foreign investment, they should be considered as a complement to an integral FDI strategy.

Third, export and technological innovation commitments should be explicit objectives of FDI policies. These vital contributions to development will not simply occur spontaneously in response to the liberalization of FDI legislation. Regional integration seems to be a strong incentive for industrial transnational enterprises, which include a larger technological component.

The Recent Increase in Foreign Direct Investment

During the second half of the 1980s, students of foreign investment were observing, sometimes with alarm, that the world's developing countries—particularly those of Latin America—were declining in importance as recipients of international FDI flows (Agosin and Ribeiro, 1987; Ohmae, 1985). In the case of Latin America, an absolute decrease in the inflows of FDI had occurred during the first part of the decade, owing to a number of factors, including both the increased country risk associated with the debt crisis and the region's impaired prospects for growth. It was beginning to seem that FDI flows would be increasingly concentrated in the "triad" regions (North America, Europe and Japan). In particular, foreign investment was growing rapidly in the United States, where an upward adjustment was taking place in the relatively low FDI levels in comparison with the countries of Europe (United Nations, 1988, chapter two).

This whole scenario began to undergo a radical change around the middle of the 1980s. As can be seen in Table 1.1, FDI flows toward Latin America have nearly quadrupled since 1985.[2] We must define here a fundamental difference that exists between the recent FDI inflows and general inflows of foreign capital into the region. The general inflows of foreign capital have occurred in most countries of the region, including those that have already made promarket reforms and those that are only now beginning to make such reforms, as well as those countries that have already achieved an acceptable degree of macroeconomic stability and those that have not yet achieved it (Calvo, Leiderman and Reinhart, 1993).

In contrast, the new inflows of FDI are concentrated in a few countries. These major FDI recipients have been, in order of importance of the inflow, Mexico, Argentina, Chile and Venezuela.[3] These four countries are at different stages in their structural reform processes and in their achievement of macroeconomic stability. Of the four, Chile was the first to initiate a reform program and therefore has the most solidly entrenched reforms. Chile has also achieved relative macroeconomic stability. Reform processes in Argentina and Mexico are more recent, but both have adopted decisive measures for liberalizing their economies and have made significant strides toward economic stability, although in neither case is such stability yet a *fait accompli*.

On the other hand, in Brazil, where promarket economic reforms are only recently getting under way and where there has been the most acute and prolonged inflationary process in the whole region, FDI inflows have exhibited highly erratic and trendless behavior. Until the end of the 1970s, Brazil had been the major magnetic pole for FDI into Latin America. It would appear therefore that economic reforms in general—and not just reforms related to FDI—as well as the overall business prospects offered by the recipient country, are much more important factors in attracting FDI than in attracting purely financial foreign capital inflows. In contrast to FDI inflows, which have a more long-term outlook and involve significant sunken-cost outlays, purely financial capital inflows are often speculative and much more oriented toward short-term profits.

Certain special factors have also played a decisive role thus far in determining which Latin American countries would receive the lion's share of the new FDI inflows (Table 1.2). The debt capitalization programs and the privatizations of public enterprises have been important incentives to foreign investment in all the countries but Colombia (which in any case is the country with the least dynamic FDI performance among the top FDI recipients). In the case of Brazil, if the debt conversion option had not existed, then that country's late-1980s FDI inflows would have been very meager. In Mexico and Chile, privatizations and

---

[2] This recent phenomenon actually repeats past FDI trends. Until the end of the 1970s, Latin America had enjoyed a privileged position among the world's developing country recipients of FDI.
[3] Brazil and Colombia have also been important recipients of FDI, but in these two countries the FDI inflows have fluctuated trendlessly.

Table 1.1. Latin America and the Caribbean: Foreign Direct Investment
(US$ millions)

	1985	1986	1987	1988	1989	1990	1991	1992	1993[a]
Total	4,277.6	3,807.0	6,531.6	9,229.4	8,685.4	8,663.8	12,470.5	14,378.1	19,839.0
Argentina	919.0	575.5	-19.0	1,147.0	1,028.0	1,836.0	2,439.0	4,179.0	6,239.0
Belize	3.7	4.6	6.9	14.0	18.7	17.2	12.8	18.1	19.0
Bolivia	10.0	10.0	38.0	-10.1	-24.4	27.2	52.0	93.0	150.0
Brazil	1,348.0	320.0	1,225.0	2,969.0	1,627.0	901.0	972.0	1,454.0	2,000.0
Chile	144.0	383.0	1,115.0	1,412.0	1,816.0	1,410.0	862.0	757.0	1,576.0
Colombia	1,023.0	674.0	313.0	203.0	576.0	500.0	457.0	790.0	922.0
Costa Rica	69.9	61.0	80.3	122.3	101.2	162.5	178.4	220.0	250.0
Dominican Republic	36.2	50.0	89.0	106.1	110.0	132.8	145.0	179.0	200.0
Ecuador	62.0	70.0	75.0	80.0	80.0	82.0	85.0	85.0	100.0
El Salvador	12.4	24.1	18.3	17.0	12.9	1.7	25.3	12.0	15.0
Guatemala	61.8	66.8	150.2	329.7	76.2	47.6	90.7	94.1	110.0
Guyana	1.8	-9.0	4.3	2.1	-2.1	7.9	12.4	—	—
Haiti	4.9	4.8	4.7	10.1	9.4	8.2	13.6	8.0	8.0
Honduras	27.5	30.0	38.7	48.3	51.0	43.5	44.7	60.1	65.0
Jamaica	-9.0	-4.6	53.4	-12.0	57.1	137.9	127.0	86.9	100.0
Mexico	491.0	1,523.0	3,246.0	2,594.0	3,037.0	2,632.0	4,762.0	5,366.0	6,900.0
Paraguay	0.7	0.6	5.3	8.4	12.8	76.3	83.1	42.0	50.0
Peru	1.0	22.0	32.0	26.0	59.0	41.0	-7.0	127.0	200.0
Trinidad and Tobago	1.2	-14.5	33.1	62.9	148.9	109.4	169.2	177.9	185.0
Uruguay	0.5	-0.3	1.4	10.6	37.7	38.6	30.3	—	—
Venezuela	68.0	16.0	21.0	89.0	213.0	451.0	1,916.0	629.0	750.0

Sources: International Monetary Fund: *International Financial Statistics.*
[a] Preliminary figures.

Table 1.2. Foreign Direct Investment, by Instrument
(US$ millions)

Country/Instruments	1985	1986	1987	1988	1989	1990	1991	1992	1993[a]
ARGENTINA	919	574	(19)	1,147	1,028	1,836	2,439	4,179	6,239
Direct FDI flows	919	355	(19)	807	674	273	465	518	628
Debt conversion[b]	—	220	—	340	159	32	—	—	—
Privatizations						1,531	1,974	3,661	5,611
BRAZIL	1,348	320	1,225	2,969	1,267	901	972	1,454	2,000
Direct FDI flows	767	114	882	882	321	618	850	1,359	..
Debt conversion	581	206	343	2,087	946	283	68	95	..
Privatizations							54		..
CHILE	144	383	1,115	1,412	1,816	1,410	862	757	1,576
Direct FDI flows	114	184	414	387	380	998	899	788	..
Debt conversion	30	199	701	886	1,321	412	(37)	(32)	..
Privatizations				139	115				..
COLOMBIA	1,023	674	313	203	576	500	457	790	922
Direct FDI flows	1,023	674	313	203	576	500	405	790	..
Debt conversion							52		..
Privatizations									..
MEXICO	491	1,523	3,246	2,594	3,037	2,632	4,762	5,366	6,900
Direct FDI flows	491	1,160	1,796	1,671	2,648	2,432	3,956	5,275	..
Debt conversion		363	1,450	868	389	85*	19		..
Privatizations				55		115	787	91	..
VENEZUELA	68	16	21	89	213	451	1,916	629	750
Direct FDI flows	68	16	21	39	30	148	161	473	..
Debt conversion				50	183	303	256	142	..
Privatizations							1,499	14	..
TOTAL SAMPLE	3,994	3,490	5,901	8,414	7,937	7,730	11,408	13,175	18,387
Direct FDI flows	3,382	2,502	3,407	3,989	4,629	4,969	6,736	9,203	..
Debt conversion	611	988	2,494	4,231	3,193	1,115	306	206	..
Privatizations				194	115	1,646	4,366	3,766	..
Total for sample[c]	93.3	91.7	90.3	91.2	91.4	89.2	91.5	91.6	92.7

Sources: Author's calculations based on ECLAC data.
Note: "Debt conversion" refers to investments in the private sector only. In contrast, the heading "privatizations" includes both those carried out in cash and those carried out via the exchange of foreign debt papers and titles.
[a] Preliminary figures. [b] Includes only private assets. [c] As a percentage of the total for Latin America and the Caribbean.

debt capitalizations have played an important role in the increase in FDI, but regular FDI inflows not dependent upon those programs have also steadily increased—leading to the conclusion that other factors have also been important. By contrast, in Argentina and Venezuela, the privatization and debt conversion programs have been the primary determinants of new FDI inflows. As we shall see later, in Argentina privatizations were carried out in large degree through the use of foreign debt obligations. In general, it is not yet clear whether the rapid increase in FDI inflows in several of the region's most important receptor countries will be fully sustainable once those countries have completed the privatization of state-owned enterprises, accompanied in some cases by debt conversion programs. To hold the interest of transnational enterprises in Latin America in the future, it will be necessary to design policies that permanently enhance the advantages of investing in countries of the region.

Sectoral Distribution

The sector-by-sector distribution of the new foreign direct investment within the different countries of the region provides a rough idea of some of the economic causes behind FDI's selection of any given host country. Table 1.3 presents the sectoral distribution of FDI within the economies of the three countries included in the study. With respect to Argentina, recent liberalization of FDI policy there has gone so far as to dissolve the FDI registration requirement, and thus there exists no complete set of official data on the sectoral distribution of recent FDI inflows. Therefore, the data contained in Table 1.3 for the 1990–93 period in Argentina has been based on the survey data from 28 enterprises located there that have received approximately one-third of the total FDI in Argentina during this period. Despite these data limitations, the figures for Argentina allow us to draw several interesting conclusions. During the 1970s and 1980s, FDI in Argentina focused largely on the manufacturing sector, but the new FDI in the 1990s has gravitated more toward the purchase of privatized public service enterprises such as telecommunications, electricity generation, gas and drinking water. Within the manufacturing sector, the automotive industry has been one of the subsectors attracting the most FDI in recent years. Another Argentine manufacturing subsector that has received significant quantities of FDI has been the food industry, in which investment has been oriented toward both the domestic and export markets. As will be discussed in greater detail later, special sectoral policies focused on both the public services sector and the automotive industry have greatly expanded the profitability of investments made in them.

   With respect to Chile, it is interesting to distinguish between foreign investment made through the ordinary legal channels (as provided for in Chilean Decree Law 600) and foreign investment made through use of Chile's debt conver-

Table 1.3. Sectoral Distribution of FDI in Argentina, Chile, and Colombia
(Percentage of the total)

Argentina	1977-83	1984-89	1990	1991	1992	1993
Agriculture[a] and mining	2.8	4.7	—	—	—	—
Gas and petroleum	24.6	5.1	—	—	—	—
Industry	45.6	44.6	13.8	60.7	10.2	27.2
Food, beverages and tobacco	(4.8)	(21.7)	(5.9)	(24.3)	(5.0)	(17.9)
Machinery and equipment[b]	(6.8)	(3.9)	(0.4)	(2.3)	(0.8)	(0.8)
Automotive	(17.3)	(—)	(7.5)	(34.1)	(3.5)	(8.5)
Others	(16.7)	(19.0)	(—)	(—)	(—)	(—)
Services	27.0	45.6	86.2	39.3	89.8	72.8
Public	(—)	(—)	(86.2)	(39.3)	(89.8)	(72.8)
Private	(27.0)	(45.6)	(—)	(—)	(—)	(—)
Total	100.0	100.0	100.0	100.0	100.0	100.0

Chile	1987	1988	1989	1990	1991	1992	1993
FDI	100.0	100.0	100.0	100.0	100.0	100.0	
Agriculture[a]	1.2	0.4	0.6	3.2	3.3	2.2	2.6
Mining	49.7	55.0	79.4	75.4	48.9	59.7	46.1
Industry	19.1	4.5	7.9	9.1	22.5	11.3	31.0
Services	30.0	40.1	12.1	12.3	25.3	26.8	20.3
Debt conversion	100.0	100.0	100.0	100.0	100.0	—	—
Agriculture[a]	64.2	24.3	19.4	15.4	—	—	—
Mining	6.8	12.7	13.5	23.9	46.2	—	—
Industry	6.4	40.7	39.7	23.4	53.8	—	—
Services	22.6	22.3	27.4	37.3	—	—	—

Colombia	1979-80	1987	1988	1989	1990	1991	1992	1993
Agriculture[a]	1.1	0.6	—	0.1	1.1	0.4	0.7	1.7
Mining	6.1	59.5	1.1	16.3	9.7	-11.7	10.4	0.8
Petroleum	15.8	41.3	90.0	58.1	53.9	72.2	60.3	47.6
Industry	69.9	-2.0	15.2	24.3	23.6	36.1	9.6	26.4
Services	7.2	0.6	-6.3	1.2	11.7	3.1	19.0	23.1
Total	100.0	100.0	100.0	100.0	100.0	100.0	100.0	100.0

Sources: Author's calculation based on information from chapters in this book

Note: The percentage distribution of FDI in Argentina for 1990-93 is not strictly comparable with that for the two previous periods. The more recent figures are based on a survey of 28 firms with foreign capital, representing one-third of total FDI.

[a] Includes livestock, fishing and forestry. [b] For the first two periods, includes electrical material; for the 1990-93 period, refers only to telecommunications equipment.

sion program (in effect from 1985 to 1991). Ordinary investments focused strongly on mining, particularly copper mining. Investments in the industrial sector are not significant and are allocated to industries based on natural resources and oriented toward exports. On the other hand, FDI that entered Chile through the debt conversion program was granted only very limited entry into the mining sector and was instead largely directed, on a case-by-case basis, into other export-oriented and industrial projects. Thus, FDI that entered Chile through the debt conversion route did in fact become more concentrated in the industrial sector (especially paper and cellulose) and in the forestry sector, as well as in financial services, pension administration, and the hotel industry.

With respect to Colombia, there was a clear shift in FDI orientation beginning in the mid-1980s. Up until the early 1980s, foreign investment had focused on manufactures for the domestic market, but the attractiveness of manufactures to foreign investors in Colombia has decreased markedly in recent years, and investments in petroleum and mining (especially coal) have now become dominant.

In summary, in none of the three countries studied has the prospect of exporting manufactured goods yet become a strong lure for FDI capital. Only in Chile, through the debt conversion program, and in Argentina, through a special automotive sector program, has FDI gravitated toward export manufacturing to any significant degree. In Chile, the manufactures exports produced by TEs still tend largely to be products based on natural resources in which Chile already enjoys traditional comparative advantages. In Colombia, the recent import liberalization trend and the discovery of oil have actually drawn FDI away from the secondary (manufacturing) sector towards the primary (natural resources) sector.

Changes in FDI Legislation

The Wave of Liberalization

In recent years the entire region has undergone a fundamental change in attitude toward FDI and transnational enterprises. The mistrust prevailing during the 1970s, which was expressed in the introduction of increasingly strict regulations, has receded and been transmuted into an active effort to attract foreign investment through the growing liberalization of all areas related to TEs' activities in the region's host countries. Although the timing of this reform process has varied from country to country, the wave of liberalization has affected almost all of them. Furthermore, this trend has not been limited to those countries that have received heavy inflows of FDI (Calderon, 1993). In some cases (Argentina and Chile), the legislative changes date from the mid-1970s; in other cases (Colombia, Mexico, Peru and Venezuela), the changes have only recently been introduced (mid-1980s in Mexico and early 1990s in the other three countries).

The modifications to FDI regimens have several elements in common, both in the three countries studied extensively in this book and in other countries of the region. The fundamental feature of the new laws is that they grant to enterprises with foreign capital essentially the same benefits—and demand from them the same responsibilities—as those enjoyed by domestic enterprises. In general, TE subsidiaries enjoy universal access to the host country's economy, with very few sectoral restrictions. In most of the countries, the need for prior authorization has been eliminated altogether or restricted to just a few investment categories. In Chile, registry of foreign investment is nearly automatic and confers on such investment certain benefits, such as access to the formal foreign exchange market.

In almost all of the countries of the region, the government now permits unlimited repatriation of capital and profit remittances abroad. In addition, the national treatment granted to TEs has benefited them in the tax arena, now that taxes on national companies' profits have tended to go down and are increasingly being replaced by other types of taxation (such as the value-added tax).

In most cases, no special incentives have been granted to foreign investors. With certain significant exceptions (to be discussed later), very few selective incentives were created for investing in given sectors or in specific types of economic activity (such as exports or research and development). Policies on foreign investment as well as industry and trade have instead been conceived of as components of a liberal philosophy that assigns no priority to any particular sectors or activities, but instead tends toward "flat" or "level" incentives. In the case of foreign investments, this approach entails certain advantages: fiscal or other competitive incentives that would attract FDI to a given host country, would also harm other potential host countries in the region. In fact, the fear of losing investments to other countries within a region, which accelerated the process of dismantling trade barriers (Agosin and Ffrench-Davis, 1993), has created pressure for the regionwide standardization of FDI regimens in the direction of consolidating essentially liberal approaches.

The exceptions to the "level" or "flat" regimens are of great importance, because, deliberately or not, these exceptions have played a very important role in attracting FDI and in orienting it toward priority sectors. For instance, the automotive sector and the process of privatizing public services in Argentina have both granted extraordinary benefits to TEs (as well as to domestic investors). In the case of Chile, the debt conversion program, which has redounded in a heavy subsidy to foreign investment, has been used to channel FDI toward sectors with important dynamic comparative advantages and has even contributed to the diversification of exports.

Argentina

The laws that currently regulate FDI in Argentina have been in effect since 1976. They establish equality of rights and obligations of foreign investors with those of national investors, and they allow the incorporation of used capital goods, capitalization of intangible assets, and unlimited capital repatriation and profit remittances abroad. Beginning in 1989, these laws dissolved the prior authorization requirement for FDI in the computer, telecommunications and electronics industries, while maintaining the requirement for prior authorization for FDI in national defense, energy, the media, education, insurance, and finance (except for banks). As of 1993, restrictions on foreign investments continued only in the broadcasting and atomic energy sectors. Meanwhile, the law on governmental reform defined the parameters of privatizing public enterprises via capitalization of Argentine external debt, and it authorized the entry of foreign capital into the privatization of sanitation services, electricity, gas, telecommunications and postal service. The new laws have even made inscription into the Registry of Foreign Investments an optional process (formerly it was required in order for the investor to effect capital repatriation or profit remittances abroad). This has made it difficult to carry out statistical or economic analysis of FDI and its effects on development in Argentina.

External debt capitalization programs have existed in Argentina since 1984. Three of these programs were applied during the 1980s, and a fourth has been used to regulate privatizations during the 1990s. Through mechanisms of this type, a significant portion of foreign capital was invested in Argentina ($718 million out of a total FDI inflow of $3.918 billion) from 1984–89. Most of those debt capitalization investments were oriented toward the industrial sector (automotive industries, chemicals, foods), and some came about as late as the 1990s. These programs contained an explicit subsidy (in the form of the favorable redemption value recognized by the government), established fresh capital requirements, and could only be applied to the installation of new plants or expansion of existing plants.

Even so, only during the 1990s, in the context of privatizations via external debt capitalization, has external debt played such a major role. Of a total $14.7 billion of FDI entering Argentina from 1990–93, some $5.6 billion entered using the modality of debt capitalization. It is difficult to estimate the discounted rate at which these Argentine external debt titles were exchanged, since they were valuated at their market price. The benefit to foreign investors and their associates (the banks holding the debt obligations) consisted of the favorable prices at which they were able to purchase privatized enterprises and the establishment of rates that ensured investors a high rate of return.

The sale prices at which the public enterprises were privatized varied over time. The first privatization (that of ENTEL telecommunications) took place in late 1990, within a macroeconomic framework of high inflation rates and great uncertainty. Therefore, the ratio between ENTEL's sale price and the real value of ENTEL's assets was very favorable to the investors. As inflation began to come down and the economy's growth rate began to recover, the sale prices of public enterprises rose significantly.

Chile

In Chile, basically two mechanisms related to foreign investment have been operating. These are the standard mechanism (Decree Law 600 of 1974) and the debt capitalization mechanism (Chapter XIX of the Central Bank's Compendium of International Exchange Regulations, instituted in 1985 and of great importance during the 1986–90 period).

Decree Law 600 is a simple law that consists of granting certain exemptions to foreign investors who operate within its guidelines. The demands of the administering Foreign Investment Committee are minimal, consisting of FDI internment and duration time stipulations (the latter was recently reduced to one year). The law specifies no taxes or time limits on profit remittances. The investor has free access to the domestic market and can opt for a guaranteed unvarying tax rate for a 10-year period,[4] unvarying tariff and value-added tax (VAT) rates during the setting-up period, and access to the formal foreign exchange market. Industrial or mining investment projects valued at more than $50 million may expand the period of tax invariability to 20 years, perform their accounting function in dollars, and contractually freeze depreciation regimens and other accounting standards. Projects valued at more than $50 million also enjoy greater flexibility in returning foreign exchange. Certain details of Decree Law 600 have been modified since its promulgation, but its main provisions have remained essentially intact, providing a framework of great stability in the rules of the game governing foreign direct investment in Chile.

Chapter XIX had as its main objectives to reduce Chile's external debt, help attract foreign capital, and capitalize national enterprises that had found themselves in severe financial straits as a result of the crisis of the 1980s. Chapter XIX operates as follows: an investor buys a Chilean external debt title on the world market (available at significant discounts through 1990) and then exchanges it at face value (minus a discount negotiated with the debtor, usually the Central Bank) at the prevailing exchange rate for a title or debt certificate from the Central Bank (or other debtor) denominated in Chilean currency. This

---

[4] Only 10 percent of investors make use of this tax stability option, since the profit tax rate is low (15 percent) while the invariable tax rate is 42 percent.

title or debt certificate is then sold on the Chilean financial market for the purpose of making an investment authorized by the Central Bank (or directly exchanging the debt certificate for stock in the operations of the private sector debtor). Nevertheless, there are certain limitations on the use of this mechanism. For instance, in the case of large investment projects in mining, only 10 percent of those investments may be made through the debt capitalization program. Between 1987 and 1990, Chapter XIX was allowed to be used for portfolio investments by mutual funds dealing in Chilean stocks (the "Chile Funds") traded on the world market (Desormeaux, 1989). When the mechanism was introduced, profits could not be remitted for four years and capital could not be repatriated until after ten years. Since 1992, these restrictions have been relaxed in order to reduce downward pressure on the exchange rate.

Investments made through Chapter XIX are regulated considerably more stringently than investments made through Decree Law 600. The former are subject to case-by-case approval, while the Foreign Investment Committee's approval of Decree Law 600 investments is a mere formality to serve registration and monitoring purposes.

During the 1985–91 period, Chapter XIX foreign investments accounted for more than one-third of the period's copious FDI inflows into Chile. There is considerable controversy with regard to the actual economic contribution made by these particular investments. Clearly, investors who brought capital to Chile through Chapter XIX benefited from a significant subsidy unavailable to Decree Law 600 investors. Ffrench-Davis (1990) estimates that between 1985 and 1989, the subsidy implicit in the Chapter XIX mechanism was on the order of an additional 46 percent of the investments' total value (obtained by dividing the value of discount notes in Chile by their purchase price on the world market); in nominal terms, this subsidy amounted to nearly $900 million. It is impossible to know if those Chapter XIX FDI investments would have been made even without the Chapter XIX discount to investors, in which case the mechanism would have constituted nothing more than a foreign exchange "gift" for foreign investors. It is a fact that Decree Law 600 investments did not decline during the period in which the Chapter XIX mechanism was functioning.

In any case, it is likely that the international publicity surrounding the introduction of Chapter XIX did serve to channel new investors' interest toward Chile. Furthermore, Chapter XIX investments contributed significantly to alleviating Chile's foreign debt problem at a very opportune moment; owing to the reduction of this debt level and to the surge in exports, Chile's debt-to-export ratio shrank from more than five in 1984 to less than two in 1990. Additional evidence of the success of the Chapter XIX mechanism has been the increase in the price of Chilean external debt notes on the world market, making debt conversion not such a lucrative proposition. In fact, since the second quarter of 1991, no new FDI has come on line in Chile through Chapter XIX.

Colombia

From the second half of the 1960s to the early 1980s, the main concern of Colombian laws governing FDI was the potential negative effects of FDI on the balance of payments and the danger that FDI might supplant national capital. The main regulatory effort in those days was to channel FDI into sectors and activities of special interest for national economic development that could not adequately be realized by national enterprises. During this period, Colombian laws adhered strictly to the provisions of Decision 24 of the Board of the Cartagena Agreement.

The 1980s constituted a period of transition in which Colombia began to appreciate more fully the potential developmental contributions of foreign investment. Since 1991, the foreign investment regime has been thoroughly liberalized. The basic principles behind the new regulations are national treatment for FDI, universality of access to Colombia's economic sectors (with certain exceptions, which will be described later), and automatic approval. For the first time, Colombia's FDI legislation incorporates explicit incentives for foreign capital— such as access to lines of external credit and to export promotion mechanisms (which, incidentally, had been on the way to being dismantled)—on the same terms as those applying to domestic capital. In addition, Colombia did away with the ceiling on profit remittances and expanded the category of foreign investment to include all contributions to an enterprise's capital, such as technological contributions, trademarks and patents. The need to obtain permission to remit profits abroad was also eliminated. The profit tax has been standardized at 30 percent, and a special 7.5 percent contribution by all taxpayers has been declared for the 1993–97 period. There also exists a 12 percent tax on profit remittances, to be reduced gradually to 7 percent by 1996.

Nevertheless, in Colombia there remain special rules governing FDI in the financial, mining and petroleum sectors—rules that are particularly burdensome with regard to the latter two sectors. Regulations on FDI in the financial sector have become more liberal over time and are now actually no more restrictive than those governing other sectors. In the petroleum sector, the present system of foreign participation involves investor association with Colombia's government. As things now stand, the government's percentage of profit-taking is one of the highest in the world (between 81.8 percent and 85 percent). Worse still, royalties and the so-called "war tax" are calculated on the basis of production and not on the basis of profits. Furthermore, in 1989 it was decreed that the foreign associate's participation should decrease if any oil field were discovered with a cumulative production greater than 60 million barrels. These regulations make Colombia a rather unattractive potential host country for foreign investment in the sector—a worrisome state of affairs given the country's clear but not yet fully tapped natural comparative advantages in petroleum production.

Mexico

The legal framework governing FDI in Mexico through the mid-1980s defined the economic sectors open to foreign investment, stipulated the need for official approval of FDI on a case-by-case basis, and established a 49 percent ceiling on FDI's share in the recipient enterprises' capital. Nevertheless, the administration of President De la Madrid starting in 1984 and that of President Salinas since 1989 tended to interpret those regulations in a liberal way. Laws passed since 1984 have admitted FDI into new areas previously reserved for the government or domestic enterprises (petrochemicals, financial services, telecommunications), eliminated restrictions on majority shareholding by FDI in many sectors, and simplified administrative procedures for the approval of investment projects. Beginning in 1989, Mexico provided for automatic approval for establishment of subsidiaries with 100 percent FDI participation in investment projects valued at less than $100 million, with certain exceptions (ECLAC, 1992, pp. 65–71; Lustig, 1992, pp. 128–9).

During 1986 and 1987, Mexico also operated a program to convert external debt into stock ownership via repurchase of investor-held debt instruments at between 75 percent and 100 percent of face value, depending on the destination of the funds to be invested. The program selectively privileged investments that participated in public enterprise privatizations, increased production capacity (versus the purchase of existing assets), incorporated new technologies, and went to the export sector. The investments authorized during that program continued to be made until 1990, resulting in strong infusions of FDI into the manufacturing sector, particularly the automotive sector. The average redemption or buyback price was 82 cents on the dollar of face value, which represented a hefty subsidy to FDI, given that these instruments were going for about 45 cents on the dollar of face value on the world market during that period (UN, 1993, pp. 85–89). As can be seen in Table 1.2, one-fourth of all FDI in Mexico from 1986 to 1990 was attributable to the debt conversion program. As in Chile, the foreign investments carried out through this channel apparently did not supplant regular FDI, since regular FDI also continued to expand greatly during the period and continued to expand after the closure of the debt conversion investments.

In 1990, Mexico instituted a second program to make maximum use of discounted Mexican debt sold on the world secondary market. The country established simple criteria governing related investment projects, opened up the program to participation by national and foreign investors alike, and assigned quotas or shares through public auctions. These debt conversion operations were limited to infrastructure projects and the acquisition of public assets (UN, 1993, pp. 90–94).

Conclusions

The liberalization of foreign investment regimens has been a trend in almost all the countries of Latin America. No longer overly concerned about possible negative effects of FDI or about the potential loss of control over the economy, these countries have come to appreciate the potential contribution of FDI to development through capital, technology, modern management techniques, personnel training, and access to foreign markets. Nevertheless, Latin America in general has tended to pursue these benefits almost exclusively through the liberalization of foreign investment regulations and not through the design of incentive systems or the negotiation of satisfactory FDI performance. Regional FDI policies have tended simply to form a part of a broader framework of development strategy changes favoring the market as the primary allocator of resources, trusting that deregulation and liberalization will by themselves result in higher growth rates and in the modernization of the productive apparatus. Within this strategic framework, FDI has a major role to play. Nevertheless, the results obtained thus far suggest that liberalization of FDI policy is a necessary but insufficient condition for stimulating FDI growth and ensuring that the type of FDI coming in complements specific development priorities. Most of the countries of Latin America have indeed significantly liberalized their FDI policies, but the new FDI has zeroed in more on the particular countries that have also offered other inducements. As will be seen later, the existence of a liberal FDI regimen acts as a minimum enabling element but is not in and of itself a strong inducer of FDI. There should be other "installation advantages" to stimulate a transnational enterprise to exploit its tangible and intangible assets in a potential host country and to share with that country the benefits it realizes by operating there.

Why has FDI Increased?

Analysts of the causative factors behind FDI have used three basic methodologies to identify these factors. The first could be called intuitive or informal, and is most often referred to in the literature on FDI and TEs. It consists of selecting what the researcher believes to be potential causative variables and, through studying correlations among these variables and FDI, assigning degrees of causality to each variable. The second basic methodology consists of the econometric analysis of FDI series, that is, a formalization of the intuitive analysis. The third basic methodology consists of surveys of the transnational enterprises themselves. The present study makes use of all three methodologies to some degree, with special emphasis on the results of the surveys carried out in each of the participating countries. The econometric methodology came into play in analyzing the causes of FDI in Chile (Riveros et al., 1994), as did the intuitive methodology, through the application of each researcher's knowledge of the situation being examined.

The national studies carried out for this book tend to agree with other recent studies in concluding that FDI policy is not the most important of the elements that motivate TEs to invest in Latin America. If the region's FDI laws had not been liberalized, there would not be the high levels of FDI inflows into Latin America that exist today. Nevertheless, in those few countries that have experienced extraordinarily heavy inflows of FDI, factors other than FDI laws would also seem to have been at work. In all of these cases, there were certain political, economic and other specific factors without which the TEs would not have shown the same interest in investing in those particular countries.

The available evidence does not suggest that the TEs are actively integrating the Latin American countries into their global production networks, but rather that the TEs are investing in Latin America as a way of rationalizing their regional activities. In Argentina, the existence of MERCOSUR has been an important catalyst to some foreign investments. Colombia's position within the nascent regional market is seen as a goal that could stimulate larger future investments. Production for the markets of neighboring countries is indeed an important consideration in various branches of industry housing active TE subsidiaries. Mexico constitutes the most advanced example of regionalization, with significant intraindustrial investments that are almost all aimed at the North American market.

As noted earlier, the analysis of the factors motivating TEs to invest in Latin American countries was based on the results of surveys carried out in enterprises with foreign capital—namely, Argentina (28 enterprises), Chile (15), and Colombia (53). Colombia, in contrast to Argentina and Chile, has not experienced a recent FDI boom; therefore the enterprises surveyed had been established in that country for some time. Even so, the survey results for Colombia are useful for predicting which factors could be important in producing an eventual increase in FDI there.

Argentina

Although there had been a fairly liberal foreign investment regimen in Argentina since 1976, the dramatic increase in FDI came about only with the economic reforms of the 1990s and the dramatic reduction in macroeconomic instability beginning in 1991. The specific factors that attracted foreign investors were the massive privatization of public services under conditions very favorable to private investors and the special programs for the automotive industry (one general program and the other related to the MERCOSUR automotive protocol).

Approximately three-fourths of the sizable influx of FDI into Argentina since 1990 went into the transfer of public assets and into subsequent investments or profit reinvestments in privatized enterprises. Argentina sought to achieve several different goals through these privatizations. First was to improve the quality of public services, which had deteriorated during the years of the public sector crisis; by specifically encouraging foreign investors, the authorities hoped to modernize the sector. A second objective was to improve the country's public finances. Third was to redeem the Argentine external debt notes. This final objective determined that participants in the privatizations should include foreign operators and their lending banks, which joined together with Argentine national groups (minority shareholders in most cases) to constitute the new privatized enterprises. The bidding specifications stipulated that the buyers should also be the service operators (which by definition almost limited the pool of majority shareholder bidders to foreign companies) and also stipulated certain investment and modernization requirements in exchange for setting rates that would ensure a basic (and quite tempting) profit level. The privatization process offered these TEs the unique opportunity of acquiring companies within a sale framework particularly favorable to foreign investors—a framework that also offered the new owners entry into a captive market promising significant growth opportunities (See Chapter Two, Chudnovsky et al.).

Not surprisingly, then, the most important attraction for these foreign investors was Argentina's privatization policy. Next in importance were that country's macroeconomic policies (which had managed to put an end to hyperinflation and ensure the convertibility of Argentine currency). Nevertheless, investors stated that their enterprises would have invested in Argentina even under less stable macroeconomic conditions than those existing since 1991.

For manufacturing companies, the most relevant group of factors cited had to do with Argentina's macroeconomic policy. These companies attach considerable importance to the prospects of the national market, currently much more open than in the past. The stability of Argentina's economic policy was also mentioned by manufacturers as a key incentive for investment.

For automotive sector enterprises, Argentina's sectoral regimen has been a strong catalyst for recent investment. In addition, the existence of an automotive protocol in MERCOSUR and the potential for exporting to regional markets have also stimulated automotive TEs to insert Argentine firms into their overall regional production and sales strategies.

In 1991, the Argentine automotive sector became protected with a system of quotas on imports of finished automobiles, and the installed enterprises have been favored with the possibility of importing automobiles at tariff rates much lower than those in effect for other agents. As a counterweight to these privileges, they have been asked to comply with certain requirements, such as the generation of sufficient exports to cover the imports by the assembly plants, fulfillment of an investment plan, and the reduction of the range of vehicles they manufactured in Argentina. Within the MERCOSUR framework, the automotive protocol regulates bilateral trade between Argentina and Brazil (on the basis of programs balanced enterprise by enterprise), establishes interchange quotas for vehicles and parts, and exempts this trade from the payment of tariffs.

These policies were pivotal in stimulating investment in automotive enterprises, two of which have foreign participation. In addition, they attracted a long-absent U.S. automotive company, as well as a large Japanese automotive enterprise that now has plans to establish a subsidiary in Argentina in order to supply the regional market.

Only two of the 28 companies surveyed orient their investments toward international markets, one a processed meat packer and exporter and the other a manufacturer of gear boxes.

Chile

Even though Chile's FDI legislation was very favorable as early as 1974, FDI inflows did not really begin to materialize in significant quantity until 1986 and 1987. The econometric analysis carried out by Riveros et al. (1994) shows that the variables with the most catalytic effect on FDI have been the debt conversion program,[5] the behavior of the real exchange rate (since much of this FDI is channeled into sectors producing exportable goods), and the country risk (as represented in proxy by the Chilean debt export coefficient).

During the 1980s, Chile's debt crisis significantly raised the country risk index. But beginning around 1985, the Chilean economy started to recover from the precipitous decline in GDP stemming from the 1982–83 crisis. In addition, the strengthening of world copper prices in 1987 and the improvement in Chile's balance of payments situation that same year had a positive impact on foreign investors (Agosin and Prieto, 1992). Furthermore, the hefty real exchange rate depreciations from 1983 to 1989 must also have helped attract investments (with a lag) to the export sector. Nevertheless, the most important factor in bringing new FDI into Chile in recent years has been the external debt capitalization program. The econometric analysis suggests that this program had a notable effect, independent of other factors, in ensuring a greatly expanded inflow of FDI into Chile. During the 1985–91 period, the debt capitalization program channeled more than one-third of the total FDI inflow into Chile, without reducing inflows coming in through the regular entry channels established for FDI.

---

[5] The effect of the debt conversion program was captured by a mute variable which interacts with GDP and has a value of 1 during the 1986–90 period.

The survey of enterprises in Chile with foreign capital has yielded information of a qualitative sort. The surveyed firms stressed Chile's economic and political stability as factors that stimulated them to invest there. The long-term changes in the country's overall economic policies (and not just in those policies related to FDI) have been an important explanatory factor behind the stepped-up FDI. For instance, the Mining Law (of special importance to the sector that has received half of Chile's incoming FDI unrelated to the debt capitalization program) established the "full concession" regimen, through which the private sector (national or foreign) would be allowed absolute control over certain assigned mining properties (Ffrench-Davis, Leiva and Madrid, 1991, p. 51). Two FDI-specific policy features that were particularly attractive to the surveyed foreign investors were the long-term stability of Chilean law and the facility to repatriate capital and remit utilities abroad.

The sectoral distribution of investment (concentrated in economic sectors based on the exploitation or processing of the natural resources abundant in Chile) and FDI's strong export orientation (between one-half and two-thirds of FDI inflows) are two additional indicators that contribute to an understanding of foreign investors' interest in Chile. Other important factors were the creation of new business opportunities following the privatization of social security and health insurance in the early 1980s and the liberalization of Chile's financial sector.

Colombia

It is not difficult to find an explanatory factor for the FDI that has come into Colombia since the mid-1980s: the discovery of oil and minerals with export potential. Although the association regimen applied to these activities is quite burdensome for the foreign investor, investments have nevertheless been significant. This fact leads one to conclude that it is not necessary to grant huge incentives to foreign investors to motivate them to commit resources to a country. At the same time, it is likely that had there been a benefit distribution pattern less biased against TEs, foreign direct investment figures would have been even higher.

As noted earlier, the enterprises surveyed were, for the most part, firms with a history in Colombia dating back at least to the early 1980s. In most, the majority shareholders are foreigners, and the companies are concentrated in economic sectors that (at the world level) are noted for high outlays in technological investments (chemical products, paper, metal products, rubber, automobiles, pharmaceuticals and electrical machinery). The firms with a relatively high percentage of national stockholders are concentrated in the metalworking sector and in the sector producing mineral products of low technological content. In general the domestic market is the most significant target market for most of the surveyed enterprises. Nevertheless, since 1987, production for the Latin American market has become increasingly important. Their exports to nonregional markets are not very significant and have increased only slightly in recent years.

For the foreign manufacturing companies established in Colombia, the main goal is to supply the domestic market. The surveyed investors mentioned as an important factor in their decision to invest in Colombia that country's acceptable and sustained level of economic growth. In terms of company strategy, these firms also stressed the importance of eventually positioning themselves in the regional market, a market that has recently been widened by various integration schemes (with Venezuela through the Andean Pact and with both Venezuela and Mexico through the "Group of Three" Agreement). Colombia's treatment of foreign investment ranks far below the other factors of positioning in the domestic (and, increasingly, the regional) market and prospects for the growth of the economy.

With respect to their future investment plans, for the sectors producing petroleum derivatives, chemicals, rubber and plastics, trade integration with Colombia's neighboring countries seems to be of vital importance. Most companies surveyed also noted that Colombia's public order situation might be a serious negative factor when they contemplate further investment.

Mexico

Recent studies of FDI behavior in Mexico indicate that this nation is the largest exception in Latin America with respect to the success of trade policies in attracting investments oriented toward external markets. In the case of Mexico, the TEs' principal target market is clearly the North American market; for this reason, the determining factor behind FDI has been the favorable outlook for NAFTA. The opening up of the Mexican economy has also apparently been a positive development in terms of attracting FDI. In keeping with a study based on a 1990 survey of 63 manufacturing firms in Mexico, the new export opportunities created by the currency depreciation, which initially accompanied the trade liberalization program in the mid-1980s, were a major attraction for investments in the export sector (Mortimore and Huss, 1991).

One recent econometric study (Ros, 1994) finds six variables that best explain FDI's behavior in Mexico: GDP trend; degree of utilization of installed capacity; degree of country risk (measured as the debt interest-to-exports ratio); real exchange rate (since a large portion of FDI is in the tradables sector); the degree of openness of the economy (measured as the inverse of the proportion of imports subject to prior official approval); and, above all, the liberalization of FDI laws since 1984.[6] According to that study, the tremendous surge in FDI in

---

[6] The effect of the liberalization of FDI policy was captured using a mute variable which interacts with potential GDP and is valued at 1 beginning in 1984.

Mexico has been the result of the following three factors (listed in order of importance): the changes in FDI policy since 1984, the reduction of country risk (associated with the renegotiation of the debt), and the economy's new increased openness to inflows of world trade. On the other hand, the pronounced overvaluation of the Mexican peso in recent years and the reduction in the potential growth of domestic demand have had a downward effect on FDI. Nevertheless, the net effect of all the combined factors has clearly been very positive.

Impact of FDI on Development

Foreign direct investment is a "package" composed of numerous elements, and therefore, it has a multifaceted effect upon development. Some of these elements are tangible assets (capital), but perhaps the most interesting assets are the intangibles (such as product or process technologies, personnel training, modern management techniques, and access to international markets). A transnational enterprise's decision concerning which of its assets to use in a given country will depend upon the TE's strategic considerations, the "natural" locational advantages offered by the potential recipient country (such as abundant natural resources, low unit cost of labor, and a sizable domestic market), and upon the potential host country's national economic policies. Two objectives of the present study were to determine the degree to which the Latin American host countries' economic policies have in fact maximized the contribution of the recent increase in FDI to development of their economies, and to articulate the policy conclusions that can be drawn from those experiences. This study has focused on the following three major groups of variables: (i) FDI's contribution to capital formation in the host country; (ii) FDI's impact on export expansion and diversification; and (iii) FDI's contribution to modernization, technological change, and the accumulation of human capital through specific training.

Capital Formation

As noted earlier, FDI's magnitude in Latin America in recent years has depended to an important degree upon host countries' foreign debt conversion programs (Chile and Mexico) and privatization programs (Argentina). In these three countries, there has been a noteworthy increase in FDI's proportional contribution to national gross investment figures during the existence of these programs (1986–90 in Chile; 1986–89 in Mexico; and 1990 to the present in Argentina). In Chile especially and also in Mexico, this FDI participation declined somewhat at the end of the programs, but in both countries FDI continues to participate in gross investment at levels much higher than before the debt conversion programs.

This would seem to indicate that both countries are entering a stage of more intense internationalization of their economies and have ceased to depend upon special programs to attract higher FDI levels. In Argentina, the privatization process has not yet ended, so it is not yet possible to describe FDI behavior in the absence of that special factor. In any case, it is reasonable to expect a significant increase in FDI in Argentina over the very low levels of the ratio of FDI to gross capital formation experienced during a good part of the 1980s. In Colombia, ever since the early 1990s, FDI's participation in capital formation has been strongly correlated to fluctuations of FDI in coal mining and in the petroleum sector.

In Argentina, Colombia and Mexico, the increase of the ratio of gross investment to GDP has been relatively weak (see Table 1.4). In contrast, Chile has experienced a sustained increase in capital formation. But even in Chile, foreign investment has been much more dynamic than total investment. Through the estimation of an econometric model for gross capital formation in which FDI is an explanatory variable, Riveros et al. in Chapter Three have estimated an elasticity of total investment with respect to FDI of only 0.06. The weakness of total investment in comparison to FDI cannot, however, be attributed to FDI's characteristics or modalities. The explanation can instead be found in the growth processes of the countries involved.

In Mexico and Argentina, although gross fixed capital formation has recovered from its very low mid-1980s levels, investment ratios are still significantly lower than those achieved in the past and are still insufficient for the achievement of self-sustained growth. The most noteworthy feature of Mexico's growth pattern since the mid-1980s has been the growing internationalization of the economy, which has entailed a strong increase in exports of manufactured goods and an even stronger increase in imports (Casar, 1993). Despite the growing overvaluation of the Mexican currency, the country's increasing integration into the North American regional market has stimulated investment for export markets, especially by TEs. Nevertheless, production and investment for the domestic market have stagnated, and the Mexican economy's total product has barely managed to keep pace with the country's population growth. In Argentina, since the inception of the Convertibility Plan in 1991, there has occurred a hefty increase in aggregate demand, but the growing overvaluation of the Argentine currency has resulted in an increase in imports greater than the increase in demand and in exports. Therefore, in both Mexico and Argentina, the incentives for domestic investment have been relatively weak. In the case of Argentina, in particular, investment incentives have been concentrated in the nontradables sectors.

In Chile, the situation has been somewhat different, with a significant recovery in the domestic-investment ratios, which during the past three years have reached record highs. Nevertheless, the growth of FDI has been even more spectacular, and therefore, the relative weight of FDI-intensive sectors (essentially,

Table 1.4. Foreign Direct Investment as a Share of Gross Capital Formation, and Ratio of Gross Investment to GDP, 1985–93
(Percentages)

Year	Argentina		Chile		Colombia		Mexico	
	FDI	Investment	FDI	Investment	FDI	Investment	FDI	Investment
1985	5.9	20.4	5.1	16.8	15.4	17.5	1.3	19.1
1986	3.1	17.3	11.4	17.1	10.7	17.7	6.3	19.5
1987	-0.1	19.3	24.2	19.4	4.3	17.4	12.0	18.5
1988	4.8	18.6	25.7	20.3	2.4	19.5	7.4	19.3
1989	8.6	15.5	25.3	23.1	7.3	18.1	6.9	18.2
1990	10.3	14.0	18.9	24.6	6.7	16.6	4.9	18.6
1991	8.8	14.6	11.4	21.7	6.5	14.2	7.4	19.5
1992	10.9	16.7	7.6	23.7	10.5	15.3	7.0	20.8
1993[a]	13.3	18.4	13.8	26.2	8.7	19.3	—	—

Sources: Author calculations based on figures provided by ECLAC and taken from information in the chapters in this book.
[a] Preliminary.

natural resource export sectors) and of TEs in the Chilean economy has also grown significantly.

Some FDI scholars have postulated that the form that FDI takes determines its contribution to the host economy's capital formation process. The trend has been to favor new investments over the transfer of existing assets into foreign hands, under the assumption that new investments imply greater positive effects on capital formation or technology transfer (UN, 1988, Chapter Nine). This belief even had legal expression in many of the Latin American countries' FDI regimes before the recent reforms, and it influenced the design of a good many of their debt conversion programs (that of Argentina in the 1980s and those of Brazil, Chile and Mexico), which gave priority to "fresh" investments. The recent surveys conducted in Argentina and Chile suggest that the distinction between the two types of FDI is artificial. In Argentina, only two of the 28 companies surveyed had made totally new investments, but during the 1990–93 period, later investments of the privatized companies surveyed were responsible for 75 percent of the FDI expended in further purchases of privatized assets in that country. Furthermore, these same companies have additional investment plans for the 1994–96 period equal to 42 percent of their original investments (see Chapter Two, Chudnovsky et al.). In the case of Chile, 10 of the 15 enterprises surveyed said that the initial investment or purchase of existing companies constituted only a small fraction of their subsequent investments (see Chapter Three, Riveros et al.).

In conclusion, we can state that FDI has made an important contribution to capital formation in Latin America and that the insufficient dynamism of overall investment in the countries of the region has little to do with FDI's impact or characteristics.

Export Expansion and Diversification

One of the benefits attributed to FDI is that it helps the host country gain entry into new international markets. The experience of developing countries has been that this market-broadening effect does not occur spontaneously but instead depends to a large extent upon the policies adopted by the host countries (UN, 1988, Chapter Ten; Blomström, 1990).

As noted earlier, transnational enterprises have played an important role in the internationalization of the Mexican economy. Not only have there been new investments oriented toward exports, particularly toward the U.S. market, but in addition, many already-existing companies originally oriented toward supplying Mexico's domestic market have refocused their production toward the export market. Furthermore, intraindustry and intracompany trade has played an important role in the favorable performance of Mexico's manufactures exports (Casar, 1993). An important element behind these results has been trade liberalization and the sizable real currency devaluations of the mid-1980s (Agosin and Ffrench-Davis, 1993; Lustig, 1992, pp. 117–20), as well as the liberalization of Mexico's policy toward FDI beginning in 1984, which enabled TEs to undertake an important role in the restructuring of the Mexican economy.

In the case of Argentina, as already noted, the new FDI's impact upon the expansion and diversification of exports has been relatively modest. A large part of that FDI has occurred in nontradables sectors whose modernization will have a positive impact in the long term upon Argentina's competitiveness through improvements in public services. Another sizable portion of FDI in Argentina has been oriented toward servicing the demand of a growing domestic market, in the context of an economy much more open to international trade than in the past. Only two of the 28 enterprises surveyed in Argentina—a meat processing company (a traditional Argentine export) and a producer of gear boxes—had located in that country with the express purpose of exporting to international markets. These investments had been planned in the last half of the 1980s, when different macroeconomic conditions existed (for instance, an exchange rate more favorable to exports) and under the aegis of a debt conversion program that stimulated new investments oriented toward exports.

Argentina's exchange rate during the 1990s has not favored exports of products other than those in which the country has a traditional comparative advantage. Nevertheless, the automotive sector's export ratio has risen significantly as a result of both the official regimen for that sector and the special MERCOSUR protocol for automotive sector products. Nevertheless, the sector's failure to meet export performance goals agreed upon with the government has been a worrisome development.

In the case of Chile, FDI has been oriented significantly toward the export sector, in part because management of the debt conversion mechanism tended to channel investments toward that sector and in part because Chile's exchange rate since 1983 has strongly favored tradables. It is also true that a high percentage of FDI is concentrated in the major economic sector in which Chile holds natural comparative advantages (mining in general and copper mining in particular). Even the new investments in the forestry sector and in paper and cellulose—although contributing to export diversification—have focused on export areas based essentially upon Chile's traditional comparative advantages.

With very few exceptions, FDI in Chile has not gone into the sectors producing sophisticated manufactures, whether for domestic consumption or for the export market. Certain investments in the services sector may, however, have indirectly contributed to export growth. For instance, the significant new investments made in Chile's hotel sector could have been responsible for part of the increase in the country's exports of tourist services. Investment has also made a notable contribution to Chile's financial services sector in recent years, and the executives of a bank included in the survey stated that their presence in Chile supported the country's export effort by providing access to an international network of branches unavailable to the domestic banking sector.

In Colombia, new investment has been strongly focused on producing exports from the petroleum and coal mining sectors, despite unfavorable official regimens in those sectors. As yet there has been observed no important new influx of FDI into Colombia's export-oriented manufacturing sectors. Companies with foreign capital are generally oriented toward satisfying the demand of the domestic market, although they are now significantly increasing their exports to regional markets.

The experiences of the countries included in this study show that it is not easy to attract foreign investments that promote a new international integration of the host country's economies. Two indisputably essential conditions for the successful pursuit of such export-enhancing FDI are an exchange rate favorable to tradable goods and the facility to import inputs for the production of exports (whether through low import tariffs or through customs refunds). Even so, Chile's experience suggests that these two conditions, although necessary, are perhaps not sufficient. It may also be necessary to institute an efficient and flexible incentive system to encourage investments that help to enhance the technological dimension of the host country's national production and exports.

Technological Innovation

International competitiveness is closely tied to the transfer of technology. The national studies have examined in some depth the new FDI's technological contribution.

In the case of Argentina, there has been a notable increase of productivity in the manufacturing firms receiving FDI since 1990, particularly in the automotive and food processing sectors. In the case of the automotive sector, the productivity improvements have stemmed in part from the application of the official regimen for the sector, which comprises investment goals (investment often being the conduit for new technology inflows). With respect to Argentina's privatized enterprises, technological improvement was one of the basic conditions required in the bid specifications. The privatized firms have also experienced significant modernization in their management techniques, and staff training has been considerable. Of course, it is not always easy to distinguish the effects of FDI from the effects of privatization.

In the other two cases (Chile and Colombia), FDI's technological contribution has been less evident. In Chile's paper and cellulose sector, the new foreign investors (who have bought into local businesses) have introduced up-to-the-minute technology. But in general, recent FDI's technological contribution has been limited by the nature of the sectors receiving the investment, especially the mining sector, which uses technologies that are already quite standardized and well known throughout the country.

In Colombia, as noted earlier, companies with foreign capital operate largely in sectors characterized by complex technologies, a labor force more highly skilled than in other sectors of the economy, and very high capital density. The foreign companies carry out little research and development, and they practically never modify the technology that they bring to Colombia from their headquarters. Nor do their activities generate large technological overflows into the rest of the economy, because they do not develop supplier networks within Colombia.

In contrast, recent studies of Mexico have shown that FDI in recent years has made important technological contributions. The manufacturing branches in which during the 1980s productivity and exports grew the most (chemicals, basic petrochemicals, the automotive industry, and various industries producing basic inputs) include those branches with a significant TE presence and where intraindustry specialization is important (Casar, 1993). Evidence also suggests that recent investments in the manufacturing sector have generated considerable technological overflows into domestic companies. An indirect way of measuring these effects is through the degree of subcontracting of parts and components throughout the local economy. In contrast with the survey results for Argentina, Chile and Colombia, the survey results for Mexico (Mortimore and Huss, 1991) showed a high degree of local subcontracting. Of the 67 companies surveyed, 37 used local subcontracting. The branches with 100 percent foreign capital tended to use subcontracting much more intensively than did the branches with mixed ownership.

From these case studies we can conclude that the technological transfer objective (as well as the export augmentation objective) should be specifically addressed in the host country's official policies toward FDI. Where this approach has been used (for example in Argentina), FDI has made a sizable technological contribution. In the two cases in which the technology transfer objective was not as actively addressed (Chile and Colombia), the results have been less favorable in that regard. In addition, when the FDI occurs in manufactures and with the object of integrating the TE branch activities into a globalized or regionalized production process (as has been the case in Mexico), there exists a greater probability that FDI will indeed contribute to the transfer of technology.

Policy Recommendations

Latin America's experience with the recent influx of FDI and the policies it has implemented in order to attract it have taught the countries of the region some unconventional economic policy lessons. Our discussion of these lessons will be organized into the following four categories: (1) the appropriate role to be played by the liberalization of the FDI regimen; (2) incentives and performance requirements; (3) complementary macroeconomic, taxation, exchange rate and trade policies; and (4) external debt conversion programs.

Liberalization of FDI Policies

A good many Latin American countries have liberalized their treatment of FDI in recent years. Nevertheless, not all of these countries have been successful in attracting greater FDI inflows. In this sense, FDI has exhibited behavior quite different from that of capital inflows in general. The recent increase in general capital inflows has been widespread, affecting countries at differing stages of structural or stabilization reforms and of differing economic sizes and prospects. In contrast, foreign direct investment has focused on a select few countries, all of which had liberalized their FDI regimens and presented certain specific conditions not found in the other countries of the region with similar liberalized FDI regimens.

In order to receive larger inflows of FDI, a sine qua non condition is reform of the FDI regimen. Such reforms have in fact already been incorporated by many Latin American nations. They include national treatment for companies with FDI; speedy and nondiscriminatory approval of investment requests once the applicant has fulfilled a few nonburdensome prerequisites; and elimination of bureaucratic red tape (e.g., by establishing a single window for all the required authorizations). In addition, access to the foreign exchange market is expedited for purposes of capital repatriation or profit remittances abroad, and basically liberal rules are adopted governing capital repatriation and profit remittances.

Even so, experience has shown that liberalization is not sufficient to stimulate investment by transnational enterprises with the characteristics the potential host country wishes to attract. Foreign direct investment is usually a long-term decision with a sizable sunken-cost component. Therefore, TEs must view the potential investment as being a particularly attractive opportunity and one with acceptably low margins of uncertainty—for which purposes the host country must offer certain additional conditions above and beyond the mere liberalization of the nation's basic FDI regimen. Furthermore, the host country must remember that it is more difficult to stimulate investment by TEs than by national firms, because TEs can always find alternative locations unavailable to local firms.

All of the Latin American countries that have been able to attract significant FDI share the following characteristics: they have a legal framework for foreign direct investment that is perceived by TEs as being stable; they have established special programs that make investment particularly profitable in specific sectors, activities or modalities; and they have reached an acceptable degree of political and macroeconomic stability.

Incentives and Performance Requirements

It is widely acknowledged that offering incentives that are too high is counter-productive. Furthermore, that particular route leads to the trap of incentive competition among countries that could be alternative locations for TEs (as the region's countries are all becoming) and in fact it does little more than redistribute a constant volume of investment among the competing countries and transfer FDI's social benefits from the host countries to the investing TEs. Nevertheless, carefully directed incentives (complemented by specific performance requirements) are indeed essential to maximize a host country's benefits from FDI.

One particularly noteworthy feature of countries that brought in FDI was that they had adopted special programs that turned out to be extremely attractive to foreign enterprises. Without Argentina's privatization program (accompanied by an external debt conversion program) and without the special programs for the country's automotive sector, the recent wave of FDI into Argentina would never have materialized. It should also be noted that these programs did not come obligation-free for the participating TEs. In both programs, the additional incentives were accompanied by performance requirements with respect to investment goals, the introduction of new technologies, or (in the automotive sector) export goals. In other words, in Argentina there coexisted three FDI regimes: one for the privatized companies, one for the automotive sector, and one for the country's other economic sectors.[7] In the first two, special incentives were accompanied by specific performance requirements. As noted by Chudnovsky et al. in Chapter Two, these performance commitments were not always met. In such cases, the national government's ability to make the investing companies comply with their obligations is crucial to the success of this FDI strategy.

In Chile as well, two distinct FDI regimes coexisted from 1985 to 1991. As in Argentina, the regular FDI regimen (in effect essentially unchanged since 1974) is quite liberal, although it does not grant to FDI special benefits unavailable to national investors. In contrast, Chile's former debt capitalization regimen for FDI offered a heavy subsidy to FDI entering Chile through that particular modality. Even so, foreign investment through debt capitalization was subject to case-by-case approval and was purposefully directed more toward Chilean sectors that otherwise would have received no investment resources. In particular, investments with external debt capitalization were directed in significant proportions toward the nontraditional export sectors.

---

[7] The privatization program and the automotive regimen are open to national and foreign investors alike. But, as noted earlier, the design of the privatization program has implied the necessary participation of foreign operators. In the automotive sector, technological factors make intensive participation by foreign automotive TEs inevitable.

As noted earlier, Mexico instituted a debt conversion program similar to Chile's but explicitly more selective, in the sense that discounts on the face value of the debt notes depended on the orientation of the proposed investments. Thus, the results of the Mexican program were more favorable than those of the Chilean program in terms of the objectives of the participating FDI's technological contribution and orientation toward the export manufactures sector.

In Colombia, the absence of special programs explains the low levels of nonpetroleum FDI. Practically speaking, in Colombia there are two different FDI regimens: one for mining and petroleum and another for all other investments. Nevertheless, the regimen for mining and petroleum, which is more unfavorable to FDI than the regimen in the other sectors, has not been designed to promote FDI in certain activities but rather to limit what is viewed as the excessive profitability of FDI in mining and petroleum. Therefore, in Colombia there has been no attempt to integrate all FDI regulations into a single industrial policy framework.

It should be noted that neither Chile nor Argentina has made use of industrial policies either. Rather, they have sought to avoid applying any kind of selective policy. Nevertheless, those two countries have indeed applied a certain degree of policy selectivity vis-à-vis FDI, with perceptible results.

These recent examples suggest the need to develop a strategic vision of the goals the host countries wish to pursue through FDI and the desirability of implementing this broad vision through the use of suitable mechanisms. Within the framework of an essentially liberal policy toward FDI, it would be useful to install an incentive system that would channel national and foreign enterprises into activities that have favorable effects upon the host country's development. For instance, the investing enterprises could be allowed special deductions on their taxable income if they export nontraditional goods or services, perform personnel training, or make expenditures in research and development. A complementary tool could be a requirement that FDI fulfill specific performance commitments (to make additional investments, to export, or to introduce new technologies) in return for enjoying special benefits such as those from the debt conversion program.

Another option might be to have, in effect, two distinct regimens for FDI in the host country. One would be liberal with automatic approval, and would only ensure national treatment and the unlimited repatriation of capital and external remittances of profits. The other regimen would apply to unusually large investments (for which it would be appropriate to arrange case-by-case negotiations) or to those national or foreign investors using the special incentives available only to projects fulfilling specific performance commitments (training of the labor force, transfer of technology not available in the country, new exports, etc.).

Complementary Policies

A stable national macroeconomic framework perceived as being sustainable has been crucial to attracting significant inflows of foreign direct investment. Reduced levels of inflation have characterized the economies of the three countries of the region (Argentina, Chile and Mexico) that have experienced the largest recent increases in FDI inflows.[8] Even so, it should be borne in mind that the impact of macroeconomic stability upon the inflows of FDI is a one-time phenomenon. Macroeconomic stability simply induces a correction of the newly stabilized economy's volume of FDI, which during periods of high inflation tends to lag vis-à-vis the desired volume of FDI. Once this correction has occurred, macroeconomic stability itself will cease to impact upon FDI inflows.

Taxation policies have a clear impact upon FDI inflows. In some countries of the region, profit taxes and other types of taxes affecting a company's income have tended to diminish over time. The principle of national treatment incorporated into recent FDI laws has extended these tax benefits to companies with foreign capital. Nevertheless, the countries need to continue examining the impact of their tax systems upon companies' net profits. Clearly, a less burdensome official regimen for foreign investors in Colombia's petroleum sector could have attracted FDI inflows even more sizable than those recently recorded.

In addition, both the level and the stability of the real exchange rate are important in attracting FDI. To a large extent, the distribution of investment between the production of exportable and nonexportable goods will depend upon the present and expected exchange rate. In the case of Argentina, foreign investment in exportable goods has been very modest, in part because of the overvaluation of the currency. This overvaluation was the result of Argentina's FDI policies, which sought to attract massive investments in the nonexportable sectors, thereby producing a crowding out of investments in the exportable sectors. In contrast, Chile maintained an overall FDI policy designed to avoid currency overvaluation, thereby helping to foster FDI's orientation towards the export sectors. Clearly, then, exchange rate policies that overvalue the national currency work against attracting FDI to the nontraditional export sector.

The stability of the exchange rate is important to foreign investors in as much as their foreign exchange earnings depend in large measure upon the exchange rate. If that exchange rate is volatile, then FDI's profitability is accordingly unpredictable, and FDI shies away.

---

[8] In the case of Argentina, it is still not clear whether macroeconomic stability will prove sustainable. But as already noted, as this stability has taken root, not only have FDI inflows increased but also the prices the government has been able to get for the privatizing companies have risen.

Trade policies have played a role in attracting FDI and in orienting it toward given sectors of the economy. The creation of MERCOSUR has had a positive impact upon FDI inflows into Argentina (which would have been greater under a policy of less-overvalued national currency). Similarly, Mexico's bright prospects for increased trade through NAFTA membership were perhaps the most important factor in its recent FDI increase. In Colombia, foreign entrepreneurs cite the country's regional trade ties as being important for future investment. Thus, in general, regional integration, by creating larger economic spaces, can constitute a strong incentive for FDI and for the regionwide orientation of production by transnational enterprises.

The evidence to date does not suggest that TEs are yet including the countries of Latin America in the globalization of their economic activities. To stimulate them to do so, the countries must adopt trade policies that are essentially liberal or that provide for duty repayment on imported inputs that go into exports. Other sine qua non conditions for achieving this objective are to increase productivity of human resources and improve infrastructure.

Debt Conversion Programs

External debt capitalization programs have brought significant FDI inflows into selected countries of the region, including Argentina, Brazil, Chile and Mexico. In Argentina, many of the privatizations carried out during the 1990s have been based upon the government's redemption of foreign-held Argentine debt titles. In Chile and Mexico, investments through debt capitalization mechanisms represented a considerable portion of FDI from 1986 to 1990.

Recent experiences show that such mechanisms, if well designed, can indeed play an important complementary role in attracting FDI and orienting it toward the desired sectors.[9] For the purpose of maximizing the impact of these mechanisms on development, the following concepts could be incorporated into their design:

- Investments based on debt conversion always entail an explicit (Chile and Mexico) or implicit (Argentina in the privatizations of the 1990s) subsidy to FDI. Because such investments might simply be replacing investments that would have been made anyway, they should be restricted to investments in those economic sectors that would otherwise not have received investment inflows.

---

[9] Several recent studies have been made of debt conversion programs in Latin America and other developing regions. See Mortimore (1991), United Nations (1993), and Bergsman and Edisis (1988).

- To increase the probability of additional investments, the banks holding the debt should be encouraged to make the investments themselves, since these banks are not generally direct investors.
- Chile's experience shows that a debt conversion program, if sustained over time and governed by stable rules, can be an effective mechanism for publicizing the country's attractiveness as a potential site for investment and thus can even help to promote FDI through regular modalities.
- In exchange for enjoying the more favorable investment conditions provided by debt conversion programs, these investments should comply with stricter criteria than those applying to investments made through regular modalities. For instance, debt conversion investors might be asked to fulfill performance requirements related to export expansion, investment programs, technology transfer, or personnel training.
- External debt conversion programs should be spread out over time in order to avoid possible inflationary effects.

Bibliography

Agosin, M.R., and R. Ffrench-Davis. 1993. Liberalización comercial en América Latina. *Revista de la CEPAL* (No. 51, August).

Agosin, M.R., and F.J. Prieto. 1992. Ajuste estructural e inversión extranjera directa. ECLAC, Santiago.

Agosin, M.R., and V. Ribeiro. 1987. Las inversiones extranjeras en América Latina y el Caribe: tendencias recientes y perspectivas. *Integración Latinoamericana* (No. 124, June). INTAL, Buenos Aires.

Bergsman, J., and W. Edisis. 1988. Debt-equity Swaps and Foreign Direct Investment in Latin America. Discussion Paper No. 2. International Finance Corporation, Washington.

Blomström, M. 1990. *Transnational Corporations and Manufacturing Exports from Developing Countries.* New York: United Nations Centre on Transnational Corporations.

Calderón, A. 1993. *Tendencias recientes de la inversión extranjera directa en América Latina y el Caribe: elementos de política y resultados.* Santiago: ECLAC.

Calvo, G.A., L. Leiderman, and C. Reinhart. 1993. Capital Inflows and Real Exchange Rate Appreciation in Latin America: The Role of External Factors. Staff Papers 40 (No.1, March). International Monetary Fund.

Casar, J. 1993. La competitividad de la industria manufacturera mexicana 1980–1990. *El trimestre económico* (No. 237, January-March).

Desormeaux, J. 1989. *La inversión extranjera y su rol en el desarrollo de Chile.* Working Paper No. 119 (July). Instituto de Economía, Pontificia Universidad Católica de Chile, Santiago.

Economic Commission for Latin America and the Caribbean (ECLAC). 1992. *Inversión extranjera directa en América Latina y el Caribe 1970–1990.* LC/R.1188 (Sem.67/3)/Add.2 (September). Santiago.

Ffrench-Davis, R. 1990. Debt-equity Swaps in Chile. *Cambridge Journal of Economics* 14 (March).

Ffrench-Davis, R., P. Leiva, and R. Madrid. 1991. *La apertura comercial en Chile*. Estudios de Política Comercial (No. 1). New York and Geneva: UNCTAD.

Huss, T. 1992. Foreign Direct Investment and Industrial Restructuring in Mexico. *UNCTC Current Studies* (Serie A, No. 18). United Nations, New York.

Lustig, N. 1992. *Mexico - The Remaking of an Economy*. Washington: The Brookings Institution.

Mortimore, M. 1991. Debt-equity Conversion. *ECLAC Review* (No. 44, August).

Mortimore, M., and T. Huss. 1991. Encuesta industrial en México. *Comercio Exterior* 41 (7).

Ocampo, J. A. (ed.). 1994. *Los capitales extranjeros en las economías latinoamericanas*. Bogota: Inter-American Development Bank and FEDESARROLLO.

Ohmae, K. 1985. *Triad Power: The Coming Shape of Global Competition*. New York: The Free Press.

Ros, J. 1994. Mercados financieros y flujos de capital en México. In Ocampo, J. A., editor. *Op. cit.*

United Nations. 1988. *Transnational Corporations in World Development*. New York: United Nations Centre on Transnational Corporations.

_____. 1993. *Debt-equity Swaps and Development*. New York.

F21, O16   L33   39 - 104

CHAPTER TWO   F02

NEW FOREIGN DIRECT INVESTMENT IN ARGENTINA: PRIVATIZATION, THE DOMESTIC MARKET, AND REGIONAL INTEGRATION*

Daniel Chudnovsky
Andrés López
Fernando Porta

During the 1980s, within an economic framework defined largely by recession, high inflation and great uncertainty, the flows of foreign direct investment (FDI) toward the economy of Argentina were unstable and relatively weak. But during the 1990s, with the turnaround in Argentina's macroeconomic picture, the inflows of FDI increased significantly and reached unprecedented annual levels. This chapter analyzes the causes of this recent FDI behavior and examines the microeconomic impact of the new FDI inflows upon key aspects of Argentina's national economic development. For our purposes here, then, the international determinants of the current FDI phase in Latin America will be considered as a point of reference. The same approach will be taken with regard to the global strategies of the transnational enterprises (TEs) that are surveyed.

The most salient feature of recent FDI in Argentina has been the close association between the new FDI inflows and the country's process of privatizing selected public sector enterprises, which began in 1990. There was an express intention on the part of the government to attract foreign investors as operators of

* The research involved in this chapter owes much to the able assistance of Laura Pszemiarower, Gabriela Navarro, and Adrian Ramos in copying and processing the statistical material, and also to the indispensable contributions of Bernardo Kosacoff and Pablo Gerchunoff, the vital collaboration of Jorge Campbell, and the invaluable cooperation of the executives of the surveyed companies. The authors are also grateful to Manuel Agosin, Alberto Bensión, Roberto Bisang, Carlos Bonvecchi, Mario Damill, Roberto Frenkel, Alberto Melo, Jorge Sapoznikow and Roberto Steiner for their helpful comments on an early version of this chapter.

the country's principal public services. The country risk faced by the interested investors was counterbalanced by the captive nature of the market and by the profitability conditions implicit in the transfer clauses. Direct participation in Argentina's privatizations by the debt-holding creditor banks themselves contributed to meeting the government's objective.

Another notable feature has been the revitalization of FDI in the country's manufacturing sector following its severe weakening in the early 1980s. Initially, the reentry of FDI in manufacturing was associated with Argentina's programs of external debt capitalization undertaken in the later 1980s. Later on, in the 1990s, the reactivation of domestic demand and the adoption of various promotional sectoral regulations stimulated larger investments. These FDI inflows have by and large focused on a few select sectors of the economy.

The present trends in new FDI call for a thorough analysis of the principal motivations behind the investment decisions of TEs, as well as analysis of the ultimate impact of these decisions on capital formation, the evolution of the trade balance, and the development of technological capacities. Evaluation of these issues will make it possible to outline certain aspects of the country's future policies on FDI. With this goal in mind, our present research has been oriented both toward summarizing the most distinctive characteristics of the overall FDI process in this new stage and toward examining the microeconomic behavior of the specific companies herein studied. The first area of interest was approached through studying data from various secondary sources, and the second through a survey and ad hoc interviews covering a sample of companies representative of the most important FDI inflows.

The official estimates of FDI in Argentina are prepared and published by the Central Bank and subsequently reappear in publications of the International Monetary Fund (IMF). These Central Bank estimates present problems that affect the definition of the aggregate level of investment and its sectoral distribution. For instance, the stock of foreign capital in the Argentine economy was last officially calculated in 1976. Subsequent updates were based upon the amount of FDI listed in the official Registry of Foreign Investments and upon hypotheses about the profit reinvestment rate. Analysts agree that the Registry of Foreign Investments has underestimated the investments made in Argentina, and the reinvestment hypotheses do not appear to reflect adequately the fluctuations in FDI portfolio decisions during the turbulent 1980s.

These same problems still affect official calculations of FDI in the 1990s and are compounded by overestimation in some cases and underestimation in others. The principal source of overestimation is the balance of payments treatment of funds repatriated by residents. Such repatriated funds—when brought in as dollars by nationals for use in privatizations—are considered as FDI for accounting purposes, even though they are not really foreign funds, properly speaking. In regard to factors leading to official underestimation of FDI, it is instructive to note that foreign participation in profit reinvestment of some of the privatized firms is larger than the flows listed by the Central Bank in its capital account. In turn, the virtual elimination of the Registry of Foreign Investments since 1990 has affected the updating of the volume of foreign capital in the country and hindered the availability of official figures on the sectoral distribution of foreign investment.[1]

These difficulties were partially overcome by using available figures on the transfer and investment of privatized enterprises and information from various other types of sources regarding the activities of companies with foreign capital participation. The survey conducted for this chapter also complemented existing aggregate data. Nevertheless, the primary purpose of this survey was to facilitate investment decisions and to evaluate the impacts stemming from the surveyed firms' microeconomic behavior. The sample included firms from the privatized sectors showing the highest ratio of foreign capital participation and firms from the manufacturing sectors showing strong inflows of FDI.

The next section presents an analysis of the macroeconomic, legal and specific policy framework within which FDI and recent FDI trends have evolved, together with a discussion of the major features of FDI's association both with the privatization program and with the reactivation of the process of investment in industry. The following section describes the survey results by analyzing the profile of the firms covered, investment determinants, investment's contribution to capital formation and to redefinition of international policy, and investment's technological and organizational contribution. The final section presents a summary of the chapter's principal conclusions and an analysis of alternative FDI policies.

Evolution and Characteristics of the New FDI

Macroeconomic and Legal Framework

Argentina has been the destination of a significant portion of the abundant FDI flows toward Latin America in recent years. After a sharp decline associated with

---

[1] According to conversations with the Subsecretary of Investment of the Ministry of the Economy, a technical assistance program is being negotiated with the World Bank's Foreign Investment Advisory Service. This program will have the benefit of participation by technicians from the U.S. Department of Commerce and will be designed to correct the present data gap. Given the Commerce Department's experience in this area, the initiative promises to yield excellent results and should be implemented as soon as possible. It would also be helpful to make use of the Argentine National Economic Census, which was conducted during the second half of 1994, in order to include information on the percentage of companies' capital that is controlled by nonresidents.

the debt crisis in 1982, the inflow of investment began to pick up again in 1985. Within a highly unstable macroeconomic context it took on added momentum beginning in 1988, basically in response to the external debt conversion programs implemented during that period (Azpiazu, 1992). In the 1990s, the surge in FDI inflows has become even stronger, reaching record levels of approximately $3.3 billion in 1992 and $4.2 billion in 1993[2] (Table 2.1).

The purchase of privatizing firms by foreign companies (in partnership with large national economic groups) has been the most outstanding element of the new FDI. In turn, the subsequent reinvestment of the profits of the privatized companies having foreign ownership participation (particularly the telephone companies) has become a highly dynamic component of aggregate flows of FDI since 1991.

The available data suggest that between 1990 and 1993 there have also been hefty investments in manufacturing and service companies not involved in the privatization process and that the acquisition of existing plants is more prevalent than installation of new establishments. Two relatively new features of recent FDI inflows are the presence of nontraditional investors (in terms of origin, such as Chilean and Brazilian enterprises, and in terms of their nature, such as banks and state corporations) and the formation of various kinds of associations between local and foreign firms.

In order to understand the new 1990s ambiance surrounding FDI activity, three groups of factors should be considered: structural reform policies (primarily privatization of public companies and liberalization of imports from other MERCOSUR members and from third countries); legislation on foreign capital; and the change in the country's macroeconomic configuration.[3] The principal elements of this macroeconomic change are reactivation of domestic demand, stabilization of prices, the agreements negotiated on Argentina's external debt, and fiscal balance.

The privatization policy not only directly attracted FDI but also generated positive signals about Argentina's economy to potential investors in other areas. Trade liberalization permitted utilization of imported inputs at low cost, consti-

---

[2] The official accounts of the balance of payments registered a FDI level of $4.2 billion for 1992 and more than $6.2 billion for 1993. These figures include funds brought into the country by Argentine investors (repatriation) to participate in the privatization process; this participation was estimated at 30 percent of the total for 1992 (Ministerio de Economía, 1993). The FDI overestimation due to this factor was even greater for 1993, because it included the privatization of the state petroleum company *Yacimientos Petrolíferos Fiscales* (YPF), most of whose stock was acquired by Argentine nationals.

[3] Between 1990 and 1993, the main macroeconomic variables behaved as follows: the cumulative growth rate of GDP reached 25 percent; investment grew 75 percent; exports grew 4.5 percent; and imports grew 300 percent. Retail inflation figures were as follows: 84 percent in 1991; 17.8 percent in 1992; and 7.4 percent in 1993.

Table 2.1. Inflows of Fcreign Direct Investment, 1980–93
(Millions of current US$)

Year	Total FDI[a]	FDI with foreign-debt capitalization
1980	739	—
1981	927	—
1982	257	—
1983	183	—
1984	269	—
1985	919	219[b]
1986	574	—
1987	-19	—
1988	1,147	371[c]
1989	1,028	—
1990	1,836	918
1991	2,439	20
1992	4,179	1,512
1993	6,239	2,984

Sources: Azpiazu (1992); Central Bank of the Republic of Argentina, Estimaciones trimestrales de la balanza de pagos, various issues.
[a] Includes privatizations.
[b] This figure corresponds to the years 1984 and 1987.
[c] This figure corresponds to the years 1988 and 1989.

tuted an incentive for TEs (because it favors intracompany trade and interbranch specialization), and contributed to foreign investors' growing sense of the Argentine government's determination to implement the structural reform program.

Regulations on FDI were established as early as 1976 to provide equality of rights and obligations with local investors. The regulations permitted incorporation of used capital goods, capitalization of intangibles, profit remittance, and unlimited capital repatriation. Beginning in 1989, prior official approval was no longer required for FDI in the computer industry, telecommunications and electronics. But authorization was still required for FDI in the defense and national security sectors, energy, the communications media, education, insurance, and finance except banks.[4] Meanwhile, the state reform law established the legal framework for the process of the privatization of public enterprises through ex-

---

[4] Inscription in the Foreign Investment Registry was ruled optional. Such inscription had provided the basis for calculating the authorized level of profit remittances abroad and observing of the terms and conditions established for the repatriation of capital. This measure lost its relevance with the establishment of total freedom of the foreign exchange market as of early 1990.

ternal debt conversion, and it authorized the entry of foreign capital into the program of privatization of sanitation, electricity, gas, telecommunications and postal services.[5]

In September 1993, a new text was approved for the Foreign Investment Law incorporating all these modifications. The new law established no requirements or conditions for profit remittance (and also exempted profit from any specific tax) or capital repatriation. It deregulated various activities still under the prior authorization regimen,[6] authorized granting of licenses for the exploration and exploitation of mines and gas and oil fields (without changing the regimen of government ownership), and deregulated the domestic and foreign marketing of crude oil and fuels.

On the macroeconomic level, the stabilization impetus provided by the Convertibility Plan (based on a solid exchange rate anchor and stringent fiscal discipline) beginning in April 1991 generated a huge increase in domestic demand. This movement—the result both of a substantial shift in consumer spending decisions and of the progressive rehabilitation of the country's formal credit system—had an unequal impact upon the productive sectors, generally tending to favor consumer durables and specialty items designed for mass consumption.

The persistence of a certain inflationary inclination, although declining, has tended to erode the real exchange rate upon which the Convertibility Plan was based. In conjunction with the economy's increased openness to imports, this tendency has resulted in the appearance of large deficits in the trade balance (which had been uninterruptedly positive from 1982 to 1991). Since it cannot resort to imposing a corrective nominal devaluation, the government has attempted (unsuccessfully thus far) to reduce the trade imbalance through instruments designed to improve the effective exchange rate for exports, by raising import tariffs, by declaring a 10 percent general import surcharge, and through various specific protective measures covering certain sectors of production.

Just as the improved macroeconomic scenario clearly stimulated the inflows of FDI during the 1990s, it played an important role in helping maintain balance in Argentina's external sector during that same period. It has been accurately said that the principal objectives guiding official policy on FDI since 1990 have been to overcome the narrowness of the local capital market and to enhance the availability of external savings and the supply of foreign exchange (Fanelli and Damill, 1993).

During a good part of the 1980s, the growing deficits in the financial services account and the flight of private capital out of the country were financed by

---

[5] In November 1991, Argentina's government signed Decree 2428, by which the country acceded to the Founding Agreement of the World Bank's Multilateral Investment Guarantee Agency.

[6] The only two areas with restrictions on foreign investors are broadcasting and atomic energy, although legal reforms are now being considered that would open up these areas.

the trade surplus and by the inflow of counterbalancing capital. But beginning in 1991, total inflows of private capital became strongly positive and turned into the main mechanism of reserves accumulation and equilibrium in the balance of payments, which had been negatively affected since 1992 by the large trade deficit. Official forecasts envision similar behavior in the country's capital account during the next few years, based on the recent trends in FDI inflows and capital repatriation.

Recipient Sectors, Company Strategies and Specific Factors of Attraction

During the late 1950s, TEs began utilizing localization and ownership advantages in Argentina in the manufacture of differentiated goods, by means of investments made with a view to supplying the domestic market. In this way, FDI led the way in the process of investment and import substitution in intermediate goods and consumer durables. During the mid-1970s, TEs accounted for around one-half of the country's production of chemicals, petroleum derivatives, metal and chemical products, and machinery and equipment, as well as approximately one-fourth of the country's production of foods, beverages, tobacco products, basic metal goods, and nonmetallic mineral products (Sourrouille, Lucangeli and Kosacoff, 1985; Katz and Kosacoff, 1989).

In later years, the pattern of sectoral distribution of FDI changed significantly. The expansion of Argentina's agricultural and energy frontiers reinforced natural resource availability as a localization advantage for FDI and constituted an important catalyst for FDI in the agroindustrial and petroleum sectors. The liberalization of certain service sectors was also a factor of attraction (Table 2.2). Between 1977 and 1989, the relatively greatest growth of FDI occurred in the mining, petroleum and gas sectors, financial organizations, and the hotel and restaurant sectors. In turn, within the manufacturing sector, FDI was channeled principally into the food, beverage, tobacco and textile industries (more than 60 percent of the total), and it also retained a degree of importance (through 1981) in the transport materials sector (Azpiazu, 1992; ECLAC, 1992).

A significant portion of FDI inflows during the second half of the 1980s was associated with implementing three different debt conversion programs. Notwithstanding their operational differences, these three programs shared the following key features: they all involved an explicit subsidy through the debt title redemption value offered by the government; they all called for FDI to be utilized exclusively to install new plants or expand existing plants; and they all established minimum requirements for additional inputs of new resources. The TEs participated actively in these programs, focusing on the automotive, food and chemical industries (Fuchs, 1990).

These investments took on a more pronounced exporting slant, which reinforced a significant structural change (begun in the mid-1980s) in the behavior of

Table 2.2. Sectoral Distribution of Registered Foreign Direct Investments, 1977–89
(Percentages)

Sector	1977–83	1984–89
Gas and petroleum extraction	24.6	5.1
Finance and banking	16.6	7.7
Manufactures	45.6	44.6
Foods, beverages and tobacco	4.8	21.7
Textiles	0.1	5.5
Chemical products	3.5	2.4
Pharmaceuticals and cosmetics	2.8	1.3
Petrochemicals	6.0	0.3
Cement	1.1	1.4
Metallurgy	1.5	0.4
Automotive	17.3	0.0
Machinery and equipment	6.1	0.9
Electrical materials	0.7	3.0
Construction	1.7	0.1
Services	2.3	4.8
Trade	2.4	4.0
Hotels and restaurants	0.1	11.3
Forestry, agriculture, mining	2.8	4.7
Other sectors	3.7	16.5
Total	100.0	100.0

Source: Azpiazu (1992).

the industrial TEs. Industrial TEs were becoming reoriented toward external markets as a result of the weakening of the domestic market's capacity to absorb their products and also because of the relative overdepreciation of the Argentine currency. Within such a macroeconomic scenario, this movement toward exports was linked to the excess supply produced by the intermediate goods industries (with international scale plants) and to competitiveness in activities based on the processing of natural resources.

During the 1990s, investment in the manufacturing industry, in businesses associated with natural resources, and in service providers reflects a growing trend emphasizing specialization in certain sectors: on the one hand, in automobiles and mining (in which the government has instituted special promotional policies), and on the other, in foods, hotels, and distribution chains (categories in which FDI inflows are market guided). According to official balance of payments estimates, profit reinvestment continues to be the principal means of capital accumulation, and inputs of fresh foreign capital may be becoming scarce (Table 2.3). Nevertheless, other sources of data reveal the preponderance of new enterprises, as occurred in the privatized sectors, and suggest that the purchase of

Table 2.3. Estimates of the Balance of Payments, 1989–93
(millions of current US$)

	1989	1990	1991	1992	1993*
FDI	1,028	305	465	518	628
Market (incomes)	77	43	37	17	19
Reinvestment of profits and dividends	597	230	428	501	609
External-debt conversion	354	32	—	—	—
Privatizations	—	1,531	1,974	3,661	5,611
Incomes in foreign exchange	—	515	1,954	1,841	2,543
Financing granted	—	130	—	—	—
Constitution of trust	—	—	—	308	84
External-debt conversion	—	886	20	1,512	2,984
Nominal value of the converted debt	—	6,343	131	3,379	3,345

Source: Central Bank of the Republic of Argentina, Estimaciones trimestrales del balance de pagos, various issues.
* Preliminary.

existing companies is the principal route by which these newcomers' capital enters the Argentine economy (Table 2.4).[7]

Correspondingly, foreign companies' share in total sales by Argentina's top-ranked industrial firms increased sharply between 1990 and 1992, and foreign companies' increasing presence within the country's largest industrial firms has been remarkable (Table 2.5). Most of this is attributable to the performance of foreign companies in the food and beverage sector, where a large share of the new FDI has entered. Although the TEs' total market share in the automotive sector has decreased as a result of the recent transfer of a vehicle producing plant into domestic hands, the automotive sector continues to be an important player within the total sales picture of foreign companies in Argentina (Table 2.6).

A recent survey of 61 TE branches, representative of top-ranking companies in the manufacturing industry, confirms this information and signals some changes in their business strategies stemming from the increased openness of the Argentine economy (Kosacoff and Bezchinsky, 1993). First, the production function is shifting toward a higher level of imported inputs, including parts, intermediate goods and even finished vehicles for direct marketing. Second, there is a significant increase in the intracompany component of these TEs' total trade and in

---

[7] It is clear, according to the data presented in Table 2.4, that official FDI estimates published by the Central Bank underestimate the recently increased activity of some TEs. One fact that distinguishes the present buying phase from other similar buying phases in Argentina's past is that in international terms, Argentine companies—because of peso overvaluation—are quite "expensive" to foreign investors. This fact helps to explain the eagerness of many local entrepreneurs to take advantage of TEs' current interest in acquiring local firms.

Table 2.4. List of Foreign Direct Investment Discerned in Argentina: Basic Data,1990–93[a]

Project status	Number of projects (percentage)	Value of projects (percentages)[b]
Executed	62.0	39.3
In development	26.0	39.5
In planning	12.0	21.2
Total	100.0	100.0
Sector		
Foods and beverages	22.7	19.5
Services	17.3	3.7
Automotive, vehicles and parts	10.0	14.3
Mining	10.0	28.8
Paper	6.0	1.4
Chemicals and petrochemicals	5.3	1.4
Textiles	3.3	0.3
Pharmaceuticals	2.7	8.0
Aluminum	2.0	0.5
Electronics	2.0	0.1
Machinery	2.0	0.0
Total	100.0	100.0
Investment type		
Business buyout	53.3	17.3
New plant	20.0	41.0
New operation (mining)	10.0	28.8
New installation (services)	9.3	2.9
Joint venture	4.0	6.3
Unknown	2.0	0.2
Rental of plant	1.3	3.4
Total	100.0	100.0
Newcomer		
Yes	78.7	61.7
No	20.0	35.7
Returning investor	1.3	2.6
Total	100.0	100.0
	Number of projects	Value of projects[b] (US$ millions)
Totals	150	3,861

Source: Authors' calculations based on data from periodicals and information from foreign embassies and consulates.
[a] Excluding data on FDI from public-enterprise privatizations and from petroleum exploitation.
[b] Includes only the projects for which data were available.

Table 2.5. Sales by Argentina's Top-Ranking 500 Industrial Firms: Participation by Transnational Enterprises, 1990 and 1992

Number of top firms	1990			1992		
	Number of foreign firms	Sales by foreign firms (thousands of US$)	Percentage of total sales of group	Number of foreign firms	Sales by foreign firms (thousands of US$)	Percentage of total sales of group
Top 10	5	4,303,676	37.5	7	8,242,596	56.2
Top 50	19	7,484,360	36.0	20	12,611,174	45.6
Top 100	38	9,298,119	36.4	34	14,531,421	42.5
Top 200	70	10,817,092	36.0	67	16,790,128	41.1
Top 300	89	11,297,112	34.8	96	17,914,285	40.0
Top 400	107	11,586,125	34.0	116	18,453,866	39.0
Top 500	116	11,670,857	33.6	130	18,674,028	38.2

Source: Authors' calculations based on data from various issues of *Prensa Económica.*

Table 2.6. Sectoral Distribution of Foreign Firms' Total Sales and Foreign Firms' Participation in Total Sectoral Sales, 1990 and 1992[a]

Sector	1990				1992			
	Number of foreign firms	Sales by foreign firms (in thousands of US$)	Percentage of foreign firms' total sales	Percentage of firms' sectoral sales	Number of foreign firms	Sales by foreign firms (in thousands of US$)	Percentage of foreign firms' total sales	Percentage of firms' total sales
Foods, beverages, and tobacco	25	3,552,218	30.4	37.3	31	7,490,216	40.1	43.1
Production and refining of petroleum	6	2,748,531	23.6	31.8	5	3,151,121	16.9	37.2
Automotive vehicles and parts	10	1,179,121	10.1	60.0	8	2,052,578	11.0	42.6
Petrochemicals and chemicals	15	1,155,811	9.9	38.1	17	1,250,583	6.7	46.6
Electronics and telecommunications	5	714,940	6.1	90.6	8	949,043	5.1	92.2
Cosmetics and cleaning items	6	372,857	3.2	68.2	7	857,591	4.6	82.5
Pharmaceuticals	13	399,501	3.4	48.4	12	617,566	3.3	39.0
Electric products	9	390,368	3.3	57.8	9	592,462	3.2	50.3
Tires	3	243,057	2.1	74.2	3	316,951	1.7	78.5
Photographic materials	3	135,290	1.2	100.0	3	213,716	1.1	100.0
Agricultural machinery	3	159,810	1.4	57.6	3	197,878	1.1	67.4
Glass, windows, mirrors	2	110,880	1.0	65.5	2	160,297	0.9	44.2
Construction materials	3	37,025	0.3	7.1	4	140,612	0.8	11.5
Nonferrous metals	2	134,782	1.2	24.8	2	136,165	0.7	24.0
Equipment for the petroleum industry	1	7,586	0.1	100.0	2	103,533	0.6	83.8
Total	116	11,670,857	100.0	33.6	130	18,674,028	100.0	38.2

Source: Author's calculations based on data from various issues of *Prensa Económica.*
[a] Includes sales data from Argentina's top-ranking 500 industrial firms.

MERCOSUR's participation in this trade vis-à-vis the participation of other external markets.

In order to adapt quickly to changes in competitive conditions and relative prices, market-seeking investments have often been followed by efficiency-seeking investments designed to streamline the particular branch's activities and help incorporate organizational technologies. Such efficiency-seeking investments appear to be on the upswing in Argentina.

In addition, certain globalization strategies are becoming more widespread. For example, FDI can be designed to make over a TE's particular affiliate so it specializes in the production of auto parts, auto pieces, and certain finished goods for subsequent export to other affiliates, within the framework of a global production and marketing network. Although this kind of strategy is not without precedent in Argentina, in the cases of the IBM affiliates (Vispo and Kosacoff, 1991) and Saab Scania, a broader movement has now been initiated with the restructuring of the automotive and auto parts industry, which began in the late 1980s as a function of Argentina's integration into MERCOSUR.

Bisang and Kosacoff (1993) have made the following observation:

> "The investments were oriented toward the consolidation of highly specialized production centers in the auto parts sector...with decisive participation by the sector producing finished vehicles. This specialization is based upon the utilization of technologies very similar to the world's best-practice technologies, oriented toward external markets in order to generate sufficient foreign exchange to produce autos with a high content of very diversified imported parts."

Based on this movement, some official policies in Argentina sought to reinforce that specialization concept, but also adding finished vehicles to the export list.

Starting in 1991, the automotive sector came under the protection of a system of quotas on imports of finished vehicles, and the installed companies have been favored with the possibility of importing vehicles at a lower import duty rate than the rate applied to vehicle imports by other economic agents. To balance out these privileges, the companies have been asked to comply with a program including export generation (to offset imports by vehicle producing companies), an investment plan, and a conversion of their operations to help reduce the wide range of vehicles manufactured in Argentina.[8] In addition, within the framework of MERCOSUR, Protocol 21 was signed to regulate bilateral auto-

---

[8] The automotive regimen was to stay in force through 1994, at which time there would be an evaluation of its results, followed by a possible revision of its content and perhaps the extension of the regimen for another period. The major provisions of the regimen are the following: (i) imported

motive sector trade between Argentina and Brazil (through programs balanced on a company-by-company basis), establish quotas on these two countries' interchange of vehicles and automotive parts, and exempt from import duties all interchanges carried out under the protocol (Todesca, 1992).[9]

Implementation of these policies has been followed by a strong current of investment in the automotive sector, led by firms controlled or partially owned by foreign capital. The vehicle manufacturers already located in the country have designed ambitious investment plans, former companies in residence have returned (General Motors) and there has even been the unprecedented arrival of Japanese companies (Toyota).

Even so, the most outstanding overall characteristic of the recent FDI inflow into the Argentine economy remains its linkage to the privatization process (Table 2.3). Roughly three-fourths of the inflow of foreign capital since 1990 has been used to buy public sector assets or to effect later investments or reinvestments in those areas. Based on a total investment stock value calculated at $16.817 billion for the privatized companies up to 1992, foreign investors have majority stock participation (41.4 percent) vis-à-vis the national groups (28 percent) and the remaining government share[10] (30.6 percent) (Ministerio de Economía, 1993).

The entry of FDI into the privatized companies has once again redefined the structural pattern of the positioning and performance of foreign capital within the Argentine economy. Just as there has been a notable diversification in the range of FDI participation, there has also been a multiplication of the actual modes of FDI participation and the kinds and national origin of foreign investors. In general, privatizations have been carried out through buyer consortia comprised

---

content of 40 percent for all categories; (ii) obligatory compensated interchange, with prior presentation of annual or multiannual (up to three-year) programs; (iii) accounting-based evaluation of each $1 in exports of finished vehicles at $1.20, for trade balance purposes; (iv) consideration of up to 30 percent of the amount of investment in fixed assets of national origin as exports; (v) minimum 35 percent (by value) content made up of products of the independent automotive parts sector in yearly exports by the vehicle producing companies; (vi) a 2 percent import tariff on automotive parts and vehicles entering the country under the compensated-interchange system; (vii) authorization of private agents to quota-less importation (at a 22 percent tariff rate) of models produced in the country and of models imported by the vehicle producing companies; and (viii) a general regimen of vehicle importation with a quota of 8 percent, 9 percent, and 10 percent of the 1992, 1993, and 1994 yearly production and with the payment of an additional 20 percent fixed tariff surcharge on top of the basic 22 percent tariff (Todesca, 1992).

[9] MERCOSUR's Protocol 21 provides for balanced company interchange programs oriented toward production complementation. Maximum global value amounts are established for the tariff-free and restriction-free interchange of automotive parts. Yearly quotas are established for the covered interchange of finished vehicles; this quota was 18,000 vehicles in 1991 and 25,000 in 1992 and 1993.

[10] Government's participation is actually lower than this as a result of having transferred (as provided for in the privatization specifications) a portion of its shares to the companies' workers and of having auctioned off another portion. As a result, foreign investors' share in the ownership capital of the privatized firms is probably greater than what is officially listed by the Ministry of the Economy.

of companies of various nationalities (many of them newcomers), local groups, and banks and other financial institutions. Although structure varies among consortia, the predominant structure has internal functions divided as follows: foreign investors retain responsibility for the operational, technical and managerial aspects of the business; national investors fulfill the administrative and financial management functions; and banks (foreign and domestic) guarantee access to financing and promote the inflow of new capital.

The presence of banks in these consortia is in keeping, basically, with one of the initial objectives of the privatization program. The transfer of public assets (one of the central aspects of reforms designed to derail the hyperinflation of 1989) was planned with the idea (among others) of redemption of the foreign debt. Most of the privatizations of large public service companies included the government's receipt and redemption of such Argentine debt titles as one of the entries on the list of acceptable payment modalities.[11] In the first privatizations (telecommunications and airlines), which were carried out within a context of a high country risk premium, prospective buyers presented open bids consisting of debt titles, together with a relatively low predetermined amount of cash.

The same payment model was used for later privatizations, although (encouraged by price stabilization successes beginning in 1991 and by the significant strides in foreign debt renegotiation) the government modified the criteria for determining the mix between debt titles and cash and for defining the effective redemption values of these titles. The conversion of debt titles into physical assets embodied an implicit stimulus (varying with the sale time and with the type of physical assets involved) to spark the interest of the international banking sector (the principal holder of Argentine debt titles) in participating in the privatization consortia.[12] To these ends, several banks formed investment companies to which they transferred their Argentine debt titles and through which they centralized operations, becoming in many cases the new boards of directors of the privatized companies.

Various indicators emphasize the significance of the debt title and bond redemption operations carried out within the privatization process. For instance, balance of payments estimates show that the nominal value of the debt converted through this mechanism (reduction of the total amount of Argentina's external debt) between 1990 and 1993 was on the order of $13.2 billion (Table 2.3). In terms of the results of the original privatization operations between October 1990 and August 1993 (not counting new investments or later changes in original total

---

[11] In contrast to the practice observed in previous debt-capitalization programs, the debt titles presented were valuated at their market price.

[12] The success of the privatization program and the reestablishment of conditions of macroeconomic balance powered the rise in the value of Argentine debt titles in the world's financial market and thus improved the holders' financial positions.

investment stock), the effective value of the integrated debt titles constituted around two-thirds of the sale total of $7.834 billion. With respect to the privatization program's total financial result (incorporating the value of transferred liabilities and the sales of shares originally in the hands of the government), the ratio of the debt titles' total nominal value to their effective redemption value was approximately 40 percent.[13]

Certain contextual differences had a substantive impact upon the development of the privatization program. The telephone company, ENTEL, was sold in late 1990 within an economic framework of high inflation and great uncertainty. The government had no access to real sources of financing following the country's hyperinflation, so the privatization program became a sort of evidential showcase to creditors for its fiscal and monetary rehabilitation commitments and providing a good faith token of the credibility of the government's announcements of radical economic reform. The ENTEL privatization was carried out rapidly, on the heels of a consumer phone service rate hike; it retained its monopolistic hold on the domestic telephone services market,[14] with modest investment obligations, and created a regulatory body with vaguely defined functions.

Despite the attractiveness of the government's telephone company offer, only three consortia participated in the bidding process.[15] The amount of the sale ($1.211 billion for 60 percent of the stock package) was 20 percent higher than the base price contained in the bidding specifications, but there are reasons to assume that ENTEL's assets had been undervaluated; for instance, the sale price was 37 percent lower than the estimated technical value (Coloma, Gerchunoff and Schiacapasse, 1992).[16]

The remaining public sector enterprises were privatized during 1992 under quite different conditions. The economy was expanding and inflation was on the downswing. With the negotiation of Argentina's accession to the Brady Plan and expansion of the country's tax base and fiscal capacity, the external and fiscal

---

[13] The debt titles tendered in the 1990 privatizations were converted, on average, at less than 14 percent of their face value, whereas in 1992 and 1993 the conversion occurred at an average of 45 percent and 90 percent, respectively (Table 2.3).

[14] For its sale, ENTEL was divided up into two geographical areas. The successful bidding firm for each area was granted an exclusive license to provide telephone services in its area for seven years, under the condition of satisfying the mandatory objectives outlined in the bid specifications. These exclusive licenses may be extended for an additional three years if even stricter performance standards are met in the first seven years.

[15] It should be remembered that even though ENTEL's privatization turned out to be a very profitable operation, investors' risk level as seen from the perspective of 1990 was quite high.

[16] In December 1991 and March 1992, the government sold another 30 percent of the stock package of the new firms on the international and domestic capital markets. These operations brought the government $837 million for its Telefónica stock and $1.227 billion for its Telecom stock (Gerchunoff and Cánovas, 1993).

situation was under much better control. Within this context, the privatization mechanisms and the regulatory bodies and frameworks were all comparatively better designed, and user rates were established in a more balanced fashion.[17] The clear reduction of the country risk stimulated participation by many bidders,[18] and this seems to have elicited offers higher than those initially foreseen by the interested consortia.

Despite the improved macroeconomic context, the government still offered significant incentives. In the case of public service companies, geographical monopolies continued to be granted to new companies created by privatization. By the same token, some of the sale contracts of the electric power generating companies included clauses ensuring them the right to supply given electricity distribution companies, thereby ensuring the generating companies an eight-year flow of sales at a price higher than what would probably have prevailed otherwise in the electric power market. Meanwhile, because of the way the procedure was carried out and because of the strategy followed by the winning bidders, only two groups ended up bidding for the two largest natural gas distributors (Gerchunoff and Cánovas, 1993).

As noted earlier, the greatest catalyst for creditor bank participation in the privatization process was the Argentine debt redemption mechanism. In turn, privatization's greatest appeal to aspiring operators lay in its offer of captive markets to be serviced under formal or virtual conditions of monopoly—a factor whose appeal was certainly not lost upon the bankers themselves. Furthermore, most of the companies were transferred to the new investors without their liabilities (which remained the responsibility of the government) and with significant physical assets.[19] In some cases, the transfer specifications even established rate-setting conditions that guaranteed a minimum profit for the new operators.

The structure of the purchasing consortia—an association of local and foreign investors—was also in response to the objectives of the privatization program. The idea was to help create new spaces for capital accumulation within an economy submerged in a prolonged recession and plagued by low investment

[17] The average prices (without taxes) paid by gas and electricity customers were higher in current dollar terms in 1992 than in 1985, but the 1992 gas prices were significantly lower in constant-peso terms than in 1985, and the 1992 electricity prices in constant-peso terms were also somewhat lower than in 1985. In contrast, the rates charged by ENTEL before the privatization were 2.5 times higher in current dollar terms and also 20 percent higher in constant-peso terms (September 1990) than they had been in August 1985 (Gerchunoff and Cánovas, 1993).
[18] Some 27 consortia bid upon the 10 companies into which the government split the public sector gas company, *Gas del Estado,* and four consortia bid upon the public sector sanitation works, *Obras Sanitarias.* Except for the Central Costanera generating station, for which there was only one bidder, there were several bidders for each of the remaining public electricity firms.
[19] The relationship between the value of the transferred assets and the financial outcome of the privatizations is the subject of controversy and certainly varies from case to case.

rates and debilitating capital flight—and to stimulate the repatriation of capital. The government figured that the presence of foreign investors in the privatizations would help reduce the country risk. For the creditor banks (active negotiators in the privatizations), foreign companies' participation in the consortia was crucial for reducing the company risk.

In addition to this effort toward gaining "external" legitimation, the government also sought to create "inward" legitimation, basically by rapid improvement in the efficiency of the services transferred. In general, the privatization bidding specifications required that technical responsibility for the operation be in the hands of companies with prior experience in the same sector, and that companies be contractually obliged to own (and keep for a stated period) shares in the respective consortia. Given the rights and obligations conferred upon the technical operators by the bidding specifications, the usual scenario was one in which the operators took on the role of "first among equals" among the partners having controlling shares.

The government did not want high-ranking officials of the former state-run enterprises to take over operation of the newly privatized companies, and no private domestic companies had prior experience in operating such services. It was therefore an implicit understanding that the technical operators would be foreigners. In other words, the pursuit of legitimation both externally and domestically was furthered through the participation of foreign investors.

It is interesting to note the higher concentration of FDI in public service companies than in privatized production or mining/minerals sector companies. Interesting also is the diversification of the countries of origin of the participating foreign capital, led by the United States, Spain, Italy, Chile, France, Canada and Great Britain, and at the same time, a relative specialization by sectors (Table 2.8). Key features have been the strong presence of European firms, the fact that a significant proportion of these European firms are state owned or mixed, and the strong presence of nontraditional investors (such as the Chilean companies that invested in the Argentine electricity sector) (Table 2.8). For many of these investors, their operation in Argentina was their first FDI experience in Latin America, and for others it was their first international investment experience, constituting a launching pad for similar operations in other countries of the region.

Because the privatization of public service companies has generated high-benefit investment opportunities, it could be plausibly argued that some sort of crowding-out process is occurring vis-à-vis investment in the sectors that produce tradable goods. Nevertheless, in Argentina this effect would appear to be associated more with decisions by the large economic groups made up of domestic capital than with decisions by foreign investors (since in general the investors are newcomers and are not TEs already established in the country). Some analysts might even make the general argument that the tradables sectors are less

Table 2.7. Sectoral Distribution of FDI in Privatized Firms, 1990–93
(Millions of US$)

Sector	1990 Amount	1990 %	1991 Amount	1991 %	1992 Amount	1992 %	1993a Amount	1993a %	Cumulative Total	%	FDI	%
Electricity					866	39.5	605	99.7	2,20	28.1	1,471	31.1
Gas					1,141	52.0			1,841	23.5	1,471	24.2
Telephones	889	60.7							1,211	15.5	889	18.8
Petroleum			458	100.0	167	7.6			1,509	19.3	625	13.2
Air transport	576	39.3							743	9.5	576	12.2
Iron and steel					12	0.6			165	2.1	12	0.3
Shipyards					5	0.2			60	0.8	5	0.1
Hotels					3	0.2			6	0.1	3	0.1
Military manufactures									9	0.1		
Petrochemicals							2	0.3	79	1.0	2	0.0
National Grain Board									10	0.1		
Total	1,465	100.0	458	100.0	2,194	100.0	607	100.0	7,834	100.0	4,724	100.0

Source: Authors' calculations based on data from the former Subsecretariat for Privatizations.
a Through August of that year.

Table 2.8. Country Origin of Foreign Direct Investment in Privatized Firms, 1990–93
(Millions of US$)

Country	Amount	%
Argentina	3,109	39.3
Foreign	4,724	60.7
USA	1,255	26.6
Spain	1,098	23.2
Italy	629	13.3
Chile	533	11.3
France	489	10.3
Canada	186	3.9
Great Britain	158	3.3
Cayman Islands	125	2.7
Australia	51	1.1
Belgium	41	0.9
Switzerland	41	0.9
Brazil	31	0.7
Arabia	28	0.6
Japan	27	0.6
Panama	22	0.5
Korea	7	0.2
The Netherlands	2	0.0
Total FDI	4,724	100.0

Source: Author's calculations based on data from the former Subsecretariat for Privatizations.

attractive to investors by virtue of the current configuration of macroeconomic variables.

Determinants and Microeconomic Impacts of the New FDI

Most recent FDI inflows have focused on food and beverage producers,[20] the automotive sector, and the privatization of public sector firms. Accordingly, the survey included companies from all three areas, as well as some of their suppliers.[21] The survey involved interviews with 28 companies, as follows: nine auto-

---

[20] From the present point onward, any reference to the food sector will also include the beverage sector.

[21] The interviewed manufacturing firms represented, in 1992, some 90 percent of sales by all automotive and automotive parts companies in Argentina, some 8 percent of sales by the food and beverage sector, and 100 percent of the sales of the local telecommunications equipment sector. The interviewed privatized companies represented 100 percent of the privatization investment in the telephone sector, some 47 percent of the investment in the gas sector, and some 57 percent of the investment in the electricity sector.

motive and auto parts companies, six food and beverage producers, two telecommunications equipment manufacturers, two telephone companies, three distributors of electric energy, two fuel burning electrical generating companies, two natural gas transporters, one natural gas distributor, and one water services operator.

Profile and Development of the Companies Studied

Foreign Firms and Investors

In addition to the new investors in the privatized firms, the sample includes five cases of newcomers (including one returning firm), two of which plan to build new plants.[22] The purchase of existing firms has been the usual entry route into Argentina for new investors, and in all cases, in addition to strategic and organizational changes, these investors are planning or currently carrying out additional investments in the country. The interviewed manufacturing firms already situated in Argentina have also made investments to modernize or increase their installed capacity or to purchase other existing firms; only two firms among this group of manufacturing firms came into the country through greenfield investments.

Between 1990 and 1993, the production of the surveyed manufacturing firms increased (in current dollars) by 237 percent, with an outstanding performance by the automotive sector, whose production grew by 315 percent.[23] In turn, the telecommunications firms' net income from sales grew by 60 percent between 1991 and 1993 (Table 2.9). In the sampled manufacturing firms, most of whose employment levels had declined appreciably during the previous period,[24] almost 12,000 jobs were created between 1991 and 1993, some 6,600 of which were generated in the automotive branch (Table 2.9). Even so, the employment growth rate during the 1991–93 period was notably lower than the production growth rate—a clear indicator of the strong growth registered in labor productivity. This labor productivity rise is explained largely by the increased utilization

---

[22] Of the 45 investors chosen for the sample, 32 made their first investment in Argentina during the 1990s.

[23] After weathering in 1990 the worst crisis in its history, Argentina's automotive sector became the "engine" of that country's economic growth beginning in 1992. In turn, the food sector kept pace with the economy's overall growth, although there was a notable recuperation in 1991. The difference between the performance of the food sector as a whole and the food sector firms included in the sample stemmed from the weak results obtained in some food subsectors in which the interviewed companies had no operations.

[24] The manufacturing sector had accounted for 29.9 percent of all jobs occupied by Argentina's employed workers in 1980—a figure that fell to 26.4 percent in 1986, 23.8 percent in 1990, and 22.5 percent in 1993.

Table 2.9. Sample of Selected Firms: Production, Sales and Employment, 1990–96

	Production (US$ thousands)					Growth rate (%)	
Sector	1990	1991	1992	1993	Average forecast 1994–96	Cumulative 1990–93[a]	Annual average[a] 1990–93
Automotive vehicles and parts	1,338,385	2,255,975	4,231,946	5,560,426	6,804,256	315.5	56.0
Telecommunications equipment	96,000	80,000	228,000	245,000	245,000	155.2	36.7
Foods and beverages	821,145	1,294,276	1,590,831	1,799,158	1,928,029	119.1	22.4
Total for manufacturing firms	2,255,530	3,630,251	6,050,777	7,604,584	8,977,285	237.2	44.7

	Sales (US$ thousands)					Growth rate (%)	
Sector	1990	1991	1992	1993	Average forecast 1994–96	Cumulative 1991–93	Annual average 1990–93
Water service	—	—	—	300,000	n.a.	—	—
Electricity	—	—	—	1,970,000	n.a.	—	—
Gas	—	—	—	1,120,000	n.a.	—	—
Telephone	—	2,033,711	2,785,904	3,253,142	n.a.	60.0	26.5
Total for privatized firms	—	2,033,711	2,785,904	6,643,142	n.a.	—	—

Employment

Sector	1990	1991	1992	1993	Average forecast 1994–96	Growth rate (%)	
						Cumulative 1991–93	Annual average 1990–93
Automotive vehicles and parts	19,572	20,275	24,686	26,171	27,358	33.7	10.2
Telecommunications equipment	1,757	1,666	1,992	2,337	2,337	33.0	10.0
Foods and beverages	7,732	10,823	11,714	12,195	11,668	57.7	2.6
Total for manufacturing firms	29,061	32,764	38,392	40,703	41,376	40.1	8.2
Water services	—	—	7,500	4,000	n.a.	—	—
Electricity	—	—	16,820	1,970,000	n.a.	—	—
Gas	—	—	4,050	1,120,000	n.a.	—	—
Telephone	40,772	35,286	36,293	3,253,142	n.a.	4.4	-2.2
Total for privatized firms	40,772	35,286	64,663	6,532,132	n.a.	—	—

Source: Based on data from authors' own survey.
[a] The growth rate calculations cover only those firms operating in the base year.

of installed capacity, although it can also be attributed in part to improved management methods, as we shall see later.

The Dynamics of the Relationship Between Local and Foreign Partners

Nearly all of the surveyed manufacturing firms have either partial or majority control by foreign investors, with three significant exceptions. In two sampled firms that produce finished vehicles, various groups of Argentine investors (investors from the auto parts sector, in one case) acquired majority ownership of the respective stock packages in 1982 and 1992, and therefore Argentine investors control those two companies.[25] Both cases came about through specific factors related to the TEs involved and to their perception of the evolution of the Argentine market. But the national acquisitions nevertheless serve to highlight domestic entrepreneurs' special ability to develop business opportunities; in these two cases, domestic investors gained control of the firms' technical and marketing operations, while product and process technology, trademarks, and access to foreign markets are still provided by the participating TEs, which function as licensers and still retain some ownership participation. The third surveyed firm that has majority share ownership by Argentine national investors is a telecommunications equipment manufacturer, whose technology component is provided by a large Japanese TE, which is a minority shareholding partner.

In the privatized firms, the foreign partners have most or all (in one case) of the controlling shares, and these controlling shares are in turn usually owned by various foreign investors, one or two (at most) of whom can function as the consortium's technical operator. The rationale behind this strategy, according to interviewees, is the investors' desire to diversify the risk, to amass debt titles (thus the participation by banks), and to have investors from countries with the ability to pressure the Argentine government in case any difficulties should arise.

The initiative to organize the privatized business almost always came from the foreign operators,[26] usually in combination with the international banks. Although the bid specifications did not prevent the privatizing firms from becoming totally foreign in ownership, the strategy of the foreign operators was (with the exception of one case) to have local partners. In addition to capital contribution, their reputation, lobbying ability and knowledge of the local business context have been the reason most frequently cited for this strategy. The technical knowledge of local partners was also recognized, but it has not been singled out

---

[25] In 1993, the two auto sector terminal companies controlled by Argentine national stockholders accounted for 76.6 percent of the unit sales of locally produced automobiles in Argentina.

[26] The exception to this rule has been some privatized companies that have strong ownership participation by a group of national investors with a manufacturing background.

as a determining factor in the decision by foreign investors to take them on as partners.

Foreign technological contribution appears to have been particularly important in the area of telecommunications, a service sector undergoing an intense process of rapid technological change. In the other privatized services, in which technological innovation is not as crucial, foreign contribution has been largely in the areas of continued investment, knowledge of the business, and the design and management of the new firms.

Two of the large national groups participating in consortia had participated in the construction and maintenance of some of the installations that were later privatized. Their representatives contended that the provisions contained in the privatization specifications had been prejudicial in regard to the assignment of roles within the respective consortia and that the national groups could easily have compensated for their lack of operational experience through technical assistance contracts with foreign operators. These local groups had to relinquish aspirations of majority control, technical operational control, and general management of the privatized companies[27] and instead assigned their executives, in most cases, to the areas of administration and finance. The national groups therefore have seen the narrowing of their possibilities of learning the full business and thus the reduction of their possibilities of branching out into new operations (either domestically or abroad) as a result of the experience acquired in the privatized companies.

Let us assume that these circumstances may indeed have curtailed the operational learning process of local investors. Even so, the fact that the foreign operators have significant stock ownership in the privatized companies probably contributes to a greater sense of responsibility for the transfer of technical and managerial knowledge, since the companies' profitability levels depend so heavily upon this transfer. The presence of experienced foreign operators also probably facilitates foreign financing for these new companies, even though there admittedly exists a profit remittance cost to Argentina for such a strategy.[28]

---

[27] In two of the privatized companies with participation by the same group mentioned in the previous footnote, national group executives perform the general management function. In the rest of the firms interviewed, the general management function is performed by personnel sent in by the foreign operators.

[28] Of the cash dividends distributed by the telephone companies in their first three years of operation, around $200 million went to foreign partners. Bearing in mind that the initial FDI was $890 million, of which only US$160 million was brought in as cash, clearly the profit levels were excellent for these investors. Profits from the phone companies also accrued to the unspecified percentage of stocks held in the world marketplace in the portfolios of additional foreign investors. Besides the profits they receive as shareholders, the foreign operators also earn income through management and technical assistance contracts—a profit channel that, incidentally, is also open to local partners to the degree that they provide management and technical resources to the companies.

Policy on the purchase of goods or services is a key issue within the consortia, because various partners (either alone or through business connections) are often qualified to be suppliers to the privatized companies. The foreign partners in the privatized companies insisted that the contracting of equipment, services, and works be carried out through open bidding,[29] without applying the first-refusal clause (through which any partner would be allowed to match the offer of a third-party bidder—an arrangement that would quickly dry up the pool of third-party bids if in effect they could never win). The local partners recognized that this is a controversial area within the dynamics of the consortia and that the last word is not yet in.

Capital Formation

Factors that Motivated the Investment Decision

The surveyed companies were asked to rank the factors that influenced their decision to invest. The results of this survey (Table 2.10 and Table 2.11) allow a fairly complete and detailed evaluation of the topic.

For the investors in the privatized companies, Argentina's economic policy has constituted the most relevant factor. The privatization program, naturally, came to mind for most. Economic policy stability and the availability of a captive domestic market have also been noted as influential factors, though to a lesser degree. The debt conversion mechanism was hardly mentioned as being a decisive factor; the foreign banks would probably have ranked it higher.

Of great significance to investors was Argentina's legislation on FDI, basically as regards the ease (that is, the explicit stimulus) with which foreign investors would be permitted to purchase public sector companies. As a complementary factor, the outlook for the domestic market was listed among the characteristics of a host country. To a lesser degree, investors in the privatized companies were motivated by their own TEs' internal strategies, especially as related to the need to be present in the major world markets.

Thus we can reconstruct the decision to invest in the privatized companies in the following way. There had been made available, on a one-time-only basis, the opportunity to acquire companies in a framework within which foreign investors were particularly favored by the privatization program and would be given the chance to supply a captive market showing significant growth prospects. During the interviews it became clear that these specific privatization-

---

[29] This is one of the requirements governing the bidding process in all cases in which the purchase exceeds a certain amount.

Table 2.10. Factors that Influenced the Decision to Invest: Privatized Firms[1]

Host country's general economic policies	24.1
• Privatizations of public companies	95.8
• Stability of macroeconomic policy	37.1
• Existence of a captive domestic market	29.2
Host country's policy toward foreign investment	22.6
• Ease with which foreigners can buy existing firms	83.3
• Public policies' nondiscrimination against foreign investors	45.8
• Ease of repatriating capital and remitting profits	37.5
Host country's characteristics	20.1
• Domestic market's prospects	100.0
• Country's political stability	33.3
• Availability of natural resources	25.0
Strategic domestic factors	19.1
• Globalization of markets and the need to be present in all major markets	83.3
• The chance to incorporate the local branch into the TE's globalization strategy	50.0
• Competing firms' location in the domestic or regional market	25.0
Host country's trade policy	7.5
• Existence of MERCOSUR	33.3
• The possibility that the host country might sign a free-trade agreement with the United States	12.5
• Low tariffs on inputs used by the company	8.3
Changes in the world scenario	6.5
• Los interest rates in the world's financial markets	25.0
• Recession in FDI's country of origin	16.7
• Other	12.5

Source: Calculated on the basis of data from the authors' survey.
[1] Each firm was asked to rank the three most influential factors in each response block in terms of their impact on the firm's decision to invest. Three points were given to the firm's first-place response, two points to its second-place response, and one point to its third-place response. Later, the factors were arranged within each block by giving them a score calculated as the percentage of points obtained in the responses relative to the maximum number of points accruable by a factor. The blocks themselves were then ranked by adding up each block's factor points and dividing these subtotals by the total number of factor points obtained by all the blocks.

related factors would alone have constituted sufficient motivation for investment in Argentina even under less stable macroeconomic conditions than those prevailing in 1992; the investment in the telecommunications services companies in 1990 attests to this fact. The main difference would probably have been the price that foreign investors would have been willing to pay, given the higher country risk.

For manufacturing firms, as for the privatized firms, the single most relevant group of factors relates to Argentina's economic policy. In contrast, Argentine laws on FDI were viewed as having been less influential (particularly for manufacturing firms already situated in the country), while trade policy (of little importance to the privatized companies) was seen as relevant. Manufacturing

Table 2.11. Factors that Influenced the Decision to Invest: Manufacturing Firms[1]

Host country's general economic policies	20.7
• Stability of macroeconomic policy	66.7
• Sectoral regulations favorable to the sector in which the firm operates	35.9
• Privatizations of public-sector companies	20.5
Characteristics of the host country	20.4
• Prospects of the domestic market	87.2
• Country's political stability	38.5
• Availability of quality low-cost human resources	30.8
Strategic domestic factors	19.5
• Market globalization and the need to be present in all major markets	51.3
• The chance to incorporate the local branch into the TE's globalization strategy	43.6
• The chance to export to regional markets from the host country	43.6
Host country's trade policy	17.0
• Existence of MERCOSUR	56.4
• Existence of export promotion regimens	41.0
• Existence of drawback mechanisms	25.6
Host country's policies toward foreign investment	16.1
• Long-term stability in FDI laws	46.2
• Ease of capital repatriation and profit remittance	43.6
• Public policies' nondiscrimination against foreign investors	28.2
Changes in the world scenario	6.3
• Low interest rates in world capital markets	28.2
• Recession in FDI's country of origin	20.5
• Other	7.7

Source: Calculated on the basis of data from authors' survey.
[1] For methodology, please see note accompanying the preceding table.

sector investors viewed as not very influential on their investment decision the possibility that Argentina might accede to NAFTA.

As for investors in the privatized companies, a very influential factor indeed had been the prospects of the domestic market. Moreover, within the host country characteristics, manufacturing investors also signaled the importance of political stability and the availability of high-quality, low-cost human resources. Of less importance was the availability of natural resources, which was singled out by only two export-oriented food manufactures.

Economic policy stability was quite important to foreign investors in manufactures, especially for newcomers. In the case of the automotive industry, the official sectoral regimen regulating that industry has had a great impact upon recent investment decisions. The existence of MERCOSUR, the possibility of exporting to regional markets, and the export promotion regimen all enable local affiliates to fit into their parent companies' globalization and regionalization strategies (factors that come into sharp focus largely for the automotive and auto parts companies).

For the privatized company investors and the manufacturing sector investors alike, the decision to invest in Argentina was hardly affected by recent changes in the overall international economic picture.

To summarize, then, certain economic policy instruments utilized by the present government (particularly privatization of public firms and implementation of the automotive sector regimen) have clearly been the factors that attracted new FDI toward Argentina in the first place,[30] but it is nonetheless very significant that, in the opinion of the interviewed investors in privatized and manufacturing firms alike, the most important factor that finally clinched the investment decision for them was the attractiveness of the prospects for the country's domestic market. An internal market-seeking strategy seems to be the one that has been prevailing; except for the automotive sector and two export-oriented food manufacturers, no significant flow of exports has been generated among the interviewed companies. Whatever the case, efficiency-seeking investments in physical assets and/or intangibles will also have to be made if the foreign investors hope to be able to satisfy the expanding domestic market under liberalized, open economy conditions (manufacturing companies) or with inherited operational facilities in a dreadful state of disrepair (privatized companies).

Investment Flows and Debt Conversion

Privatized Companies. Between 1990 and 1993, the sampled privatized companies had a combined FDI level of $3.842 billion. Of this sum, $2.195 billion went into the purchase of the respective firms, and the remaining $1.647 billion went into post-privatization investments. Except for the water service company *Aguas Argentinas*[31] (for which payment was not required) and the fuel-burning electricity generating companies (which were paid for in cash), the major part of the payment was made by means of Argentine external debt titles (Table 2.12).

In telecommunications, debt conversion was in fact a key factor in the original investment decision. In the later privatizations, there usually were different views with regard to the debt conversion mechanism between the technical operators (who held no debt titles and were therefore indifferent as to whether to

---

[30] The positive aspect of this element of attraction of the mentioned policy should be viewed alongside the policy's eventual costs, principally in fiscal terms and in terms of consumer income. The effects on consumer income are discussed later in this chapter. As for the privatizations' fiscal effect, it has been found by Gerchunoff and Cánovas (1993) to be a positive one.

[31] Privatization of the sanitation service *(Obras Sanitarias)* was not carried out through the sale of stocks, but rather by granting the concessions for water production and distribution and for sewage collection to the consortium offering the greatest discount on rates, consistent with the technical plan.

Table 2.12. Sample of Selected Firms: Total Investment and FDI, 1990–96
(Thousands of US$)

Sector	1990	1991	1992	1993	Cumulative 1990–93	Forecast average 1994–96
Automotive vehicles and parts						
Total investment	154,736	254,853	149,796	251,122	810,507	405,909
FDI	77,626	119,626	72,993	111,703	381,948	168,253
Telecommunications equipment						
Total investment	4,000	10,000	24,000	10,000	48,000	n.a.
FDI	4,000	7,960	16,850	10,000	38,820	n.a.
Foods and beverages						
Total investment	59,191	93,814	128,901	176,745	458,651	192,706
FDI	61,291	85,291	121,214	236,701	504,497	251,278
Subtotal manufactures						
Total investment	217,927	358,667	302,697	437,867	1,317,158	598,615
FDI	142,917	212,877	211,067	358,404	925,265	419,531
Water services						
Total investment	—	—	—	90,000	90,000	200,000
FDI	—	—	—	45,360	45,360	100,800
Electricity						
Total investment	—	—	1,266,080	294,300	1,560,380	298,667
FDI	—	—	794,390	119,439	913,829	122,380
• Inv. to buy firm	—	—	788,150	—	788,150	—
through capitalization of debt	—	—	590,060	—	590,060	—
• Later investment	—	—	6,240	119,439	125,679	122,380

Gas						
Total investment	—	—	520,080	115,600	635,680	171,700
FDI	—	—	518,390	50,766	569,156	78,318
• Inv. to buy firm	—	—	518,390	—	518,390	—
through capitalization of debt			408,270		408,270	
• Later investment	—	—	—	50,766	50,766	78,318
Telephone						
Total investment	1,211,000	305,000	1,202,000	1,642,000	4,360,000	1,352,000
FDI	889,000	138,125	543,900	742,965	2,313,990	611,950
• Inv. to buy firm	889,000	—	—	—	889,000	—
through capitalization of firm	759,980				759,980	
• Later investment	—	138,125	543,900	742,965	1,424,990	611,950
Subtotal privatized firms						
Total investment	1,211,000	305,000	2,988,160	2,141,900	6,646,060	2,022,367
FDI	889,000	138,125	1,856,680	958,530	3,842,335	913,448
• Inv. to buy firm	889,000	—	1,306,540	—	2,195,540	—
through capitalization of debt	759,980		998,330		1,758,310	
• Later investment	—	138,125	550,140	958,530	1,646,795	913,448
Total						
Total investment	1,428,927	663,667	3,290,857	2,579,767	7,963,218	2,620,982
FDI	1,031,917	351,002	2,067,747	1,316,934	4,767,600	1,332,979

Source: Calculated on the basis of data from authors' surveys.

pay cash for the company shares or to buy them at the market price)[32] and the banks (for whom the debt conversion mechanism was quite advantageous).[33]

Most of the later investments by the privatized firms were financed through profit reinvestment and, to a lesser degree, through taking on indebtedness, both local and foreign (for instance, through negotiable debt instruments). In the initial phase, such investments absorbed a large part of the companies' profits. Nevertheless, if loan acquisition conditions continue to be good, it is reasonable to assume that as the companies' investment plans are implemented, the flow of remitted benefits will begin to grow significantly. In view of the linkages between the service providers and their suppliers, part of these profit transfers could be channeled through the pricing arrangements for inputs, equipment and services, and through technical assistance contracts.

The investment-to-sales ratio was on the rise between 1991 and 1993. This ratio is predicted to stabilize at around 30 percent, with a higher ratio for the telephone and water services companies and a lower ratio for the electricity and natural gas companies (Table 2.13). The survey data indicate that, on the average, around 60 percent of the value of current and foreseen investments will involve domestic sourcing, with a considerable impact upon the domestic supply of machinery, equipment, transport materials and construction works.

The cumulative FDI in telecommunications following the privatization has greatly exceeded ENTEL's purchase price and reached a high of $743 million in 1993.[34] It is the companies in the telecommunications services sector that are planning the highest levels of investment for the 1994–96 period (Table 2.12). The investment plan now being implemented is designed to extend the network,

---

[32] In any case, operators—when asked if they would have carried out the investment if the debt capitalization program had not been in place—generally tended to respond that their decision would have depended upon the sale price of the firm to be privatized.

[33] The liquidation on the secondary market of the titles held by the banks in amounts equivalent to the amounts redeemed during the privatization process would have made the titles' market value fall even lower. Furthermore, by utilizing the debt capitalization program to acquire Argentine companies, the title-holding banks did not increase their financial exposure in Argentina; they also benefited from a difference between the titles' effective value on the world market and the slightly larger value set by the government of Argentina. And in the case of the privatization of ENTEL, the world market value of these titles had actually been quite low indeed, because of associated noncompliance and delays.

[34] In 1992, the telecommunications sector's investment plan finally began to speed up. The number of phone lines installed during 1991 had been the lowest since 1984, and 1991 had been one of the three years since 1976 with the lowest telecommunications investment levels (FIEL, 1992). The postponement of investments and the financial utilization of profits helped provide the funds necessary for compliance with the physical investment program without the partners' having to bring in additional capital.

Table 2.13. Sample of Selected Firms: Investment Coefficients[a], 1990–96
(Percentages)

Sector	1990	1991	1992	1993	Forecast of average annual coefficient 1994–96[b]
Automotive vehicles and parts	10.6	11.3	3.5	4.5	5.7
Telecommunications equipment	4.2	12.5	10.5	4.1	n.a.
Foods and beverages	7.2	8.1	9.8	10.0	n.a.
Subtotal manufacturers	9.1	9.9	5.0	5.8	6.6
Water services	—	—	—	30.0	66.7
Electricity	—	—	—	11.3	13.1
Gas	—	—	—	10.3	15.3
Telephone	—	15.0	43.1	50.5	41.6
Subtotal privatized firms	—	15.0	43.1	31.9	29.7
Total	9.1	11.7	17.0	17.7	16.4

Source: Calculated on the basis of data from authors' survey.
[a] Calculated as the ratio between investments and production (manufacturing firms) or between investments and sales (privatized companies).
[b] Because no sales projection figures were available for the privatized companies, we have assumed in calculating the future investment coefficients that the privatized companies will maintain the same level of sales as in 1993.

enhance computerization and improve service quality, and has already placed these firms ahead of the goals stipulated in the bid specifications.

The bid specifications established different requirements for the companies that were subsequently privatized. In the electricity and natural gas sectors they established mandatory service quality and dependability and safety goals, which for the latter even included related investment amounts that could be made obligatory by the official regulatory body. In addition, the rates established were deemed to be sufficient to permit the companies to carry out, in each stage of the service, certain investments in system efficiency and expansion (which, in the case of the gas companies, appear quantified as optional investments).

The two principal electrical distribution companies made investments in 1993 toward network improvements, meter installation, and the like, with the fundamental objective of reducing the significant losses suffered that year ($65 million by one company and $66 million by the other) from energy theft. Meanwhile, the fuel-burning electrical power stations are moving ahead with their $400 million 1992–95 investment plan targeted to repair equipment, enhancing availability and efficiency. In addition to these rehabilitative investments, one electric power station's owners initiated in 1993 the construction of a new turboelectric power generating plant; this is the first case of a new post-privatization investment made by an interviewed privatized firm.[35]

The natural gas transporters have undertaken a $140 million investment plan to increase their transport capacity and satisfy the excess demand that now exists in the market. Meanwhile, the natural gas distribution sector also made some investments in 1993, designed primarily to increase the gas distribution system's efficiency, but has not yet undertaken important expansion works. In fact, some electricity and gas firms appear to be running behind on their investment commitments. For this reason, the natural gas sector's regulatory body has called for the deposit of funds to cover the tardy investment works in a special account where they will be held as security until the firms show that the funds are being used for pending investments.

In the case of the water services firms, the bid specifications comprised certain investment goals in physical assets, including a 30-year, $4 billion investment plan, $1 billion of which was to be invested during the first five years. The 1993 investments were designed essentially to help alleviate the cumulative national shortfall in water supply and to make the water system more reliable, as a foundation for undertaking the larger-scale works planned for the coming years.

In the telecommunications services sector the expected profitability of expanding business is the main engine fueling the investment program. But in the electricity and natural gas sectors it is doubtful that the companies would have freely taken on their own large-scale investment programs without specific mandatory investment and service quality goals and obligations. It is not really surprising that the only investments made have been those designed to help gain solvent new clients, reduce operating costs, or enhance service provision capacity.

Manufacturing Firms. The FDI of the surveyed manufacturing firms in the 1990–93 period was $925 million (Table 2.12). For marketing reasons, foreign investors who had acquired existing firms were reluctant to provide interviewers with the data necessary for calculating the cost of the existing firms versus the amount of total later investment flows. Nevertheless, it can be estimated that of the total $925 million in FDI between 1990 and 1993, only 20 percent was absorbed by the acquisition of existing firms. With respect to the investment coefficient, it is seen to be quite a bit lower for the surveyed manufacturing firms than for the surveyed privatized firms, and it actually shows a down-

---

[35] Some of the foreign investors in our sample who bought Argentine electric companies continued to invest in additional electricity sector privatizations. The surveyed foreign investor in the gas distributorship has, after several months of operating in Argentina, acquired 45 percent of an earlier-privatized electricity-generating station.

ward overall trend for the manufacturing firms, fundamentally because of the behavior of the automotive companies, for which production grew faster than the amounts invested (Table 2.13).

The 1991 data reveal the importance of FDI stemming from the installation of a new plant with state-of-the-art technology, built by an auto producer to manufacture transmissions for motor vehicles destined chiefly for export. This investment was planned in 1988, within an export-friendly Argentine economic context, as a function of the parent firm's international and subregional strategy. The investment is still viable, but for reasons somewhat different from the original ones, as we shall later explain in more detail.

The other greenfield investment among our sampled manufacturing companies was in the food sector: a modern meat-processing plant that began operations in 1993. This is a project designed primarily for the export of value-added meat products; it was planned during the second half of the 1980s and construction began in 1990. Despite lowered profitability under current macroeconomic conditions, this plant provides its parent company with an improved position for competing for sales of processed meat products in the traditional markets for such goods, as well as in several new markets, such as Brazil and certain Asian countries. Even so, the difficult domestic and international situation faced by this subsector since 1991 has made the parent company repeatedly doubt whether to continue its investment in the plant.

These two greenfield investments are the sample's only clearly export-oriented investments, and they were carried out in part by means of the external debt conversion programs in effect during the 1980s. According to the interviewed companies, the investment in the meat-processing plant would probably have been on a smaller scale without the debt conversion program. For the automotive plant, the debt conversion program was an important but not crucial factor in the investment decision.

The new FDI oriented toward acquisition of manufacturing enterprises became active in late 1991, when macroeconomic indicators had noticeably improved and the domestic market (especially for consumer goods) was clearly in a stage of expansion.

The companies producing vehicles (and an auto parts producer affiliated with one of these companies) were the leaders in investments made by the interviewed manufacturing firms during the 1990–93 period. A large part of these investments went into projects designed for the production of auto parts on a supranational scale, and the rest went into improvements in their production capacity and the introduction of new vehicle models. The investments already made and those projected from 1994 onwards are based upon the evolution and prospects of the domestic market, the pertinent investment commitments outlined in the official regimen for the automotive sector, and by MERCOSUR's Protocol 21. Meanwhile, the sample's other (independent) auto part manufacturers have made very small investments in tools and machinery but have been active in the introduction of new fabrication technologies.

Among the surveyed food manufacturers, investments have grown since 1991, and in 1994 a strong investment surge is expected with construction of two projected new plants. Except for the meat-processing plant described earlier and for a TE traditionally oriented toward agricultural commodity exports, recent investments by the sampled food manufacturers have been motivated by the rapid growth of Argentina's domestic market and by the perceived advantages of supplying that market with local production and even of substituting finished food product imports, as has been occurring since 1991.

The interviewed manufacturers of telecommunications equipment, for their part, had already made investments during the 1980s to produce switching stations and had idle capacity at the time of the survey. Thus, these producers' investment levels during the 1990s were not very high. The growing domestic market was the principal motivating factor behind their recent investments.

Foreign Trade

Findings regarding the surveyed manufacturing companies' export propensity run counter to certain habitual and historical trends in the respective sectors.

For instance, the automotive sector—which in Argentina has been oriented almost exclusively toward the domestic market—has shown an almost 20 percent export coefficient during the 1990s. Meanwhile, the new investors in the food industry—a sector that because of the country's relative endowment in various food-related factors could have been expected to attract export-oriented FDI—have chosen to direct their production efforts preferentially toward the local market. The new export-oriented meat-processing plant is the only new FDI project based on the country's existing natural comparative advantages, and even it was conceived of in a macroeconomic context different from today's, particularly as regards the exchange rate.

During the 1990–93 period, there was an increase in the interviewed manufacturing firms' exports (from $750 million to $1.637 billion) and an even sharper increase in their imports (from $239 million to $1.633 billion). As a result, their trade balance declined, even becoming negative in 1992, with a slightly positive figure recorded for 1993 (Table 2.14).

Very high levels of intracompany trade have been recorded among the surveyed manufacturing firms, especially of imports. A growth trend has emerged in the importance of intracompany trade with affiliates in other MERCOSUR countries (Table 2.15), paralleling the increased importance of Brazil and MERCOSUR as recipients of our sampled firms' exports (Table 2.16).

Exports are growing in all of the sectors covered in the survey. This stems largely from the official automotive sector regimen and from the evolution of

Table 2.14. Sample of Selected Firms: Foreign Trade, 1990–96
(Thousands of US$)

Exports

Sector	1990	1991	1992	1993	Average forecast 1994–96
Automotive vehicles and parts	139,244	229,294	429,092	739,510	1,532,882
Telecommunications equipment	82	4,100	5,650	7,500	7,500
Foods and beverages	610,515	693,015	766,873	889,893	946,448
Total	749,841	926,409	1,201,615	1,636,903	2,486,830

Imports

Sector	1990	1991	1992	1993	Average forecast 1994–96
Automotive vehicles and parts	205,519	645,392	1,507,066	1,403,004	1,928,764
Telecommunications equipment	17,600	26,700	46,300	75,000	75,000
Foods and beverages	15,947	60,868	110,235	154,938	183,597
Total	239,066	732,960	1,663,601	1,632,942	2,187,361

Trade Balance

Sector	1990	1991	1992	1993	Average forecast 1994–96
Automotive vehicles and parts	-66,275	-416,098	-1,077,974	-663,494	-395,882
Telecommunications equipment	-17,518	-22,700	-40,950	-68,000	-68,000
Foods and beverages	594,568	632,147	656,638	734,955	762,851
Total	510,775	193,349	-462,286	3,461	298,969

Source: Calculated on the basis of data from authors' survey.

Table 2.15. Sample of Selected Firms: Intrafirm Trade,[1] 1990–92

(Percentages)

Total

Sector	Exports			Imports		
	1990	1991	1992	1990	1991	1992
Automotive vehicles and parts	85.9	91.0	93.7	97.2	94.4	94.4
Telecommunications equipment	100.0	95.4	100.0	96.4	97.1	83.6
Foods and beverages	68.5	64.5	64.9	26.4	16.6	31.7
Total	71.7	71.2	75.4	92.5	88.0	88.1

With their MERCOSUR Affiliates

Sector	Exports			Imports		
	1990	1991	1992	1990	1991	1992
Automotive vehicles and parts	31.4	47.9	66.0	38.4	51.1	56.4
Telecommunications equipment	—	7.6	2.1	—	—	—
Foods and beverages	0.9	1.3	0.1	1.6	2.5	5.3
Total	6.6	12.8	23.7	32.2	45.1	49.8

Source: Calculated on the basis of data from authors' survey.
[1] Percentages are calculated on the basis of firms' total exports.

Table 2.16. Sample of Selected Firms: Destination of Exports, 1990–92
(Percentages)

Sector	Brazil			MERCOSUR			Rest of Latin America	U.S.A.	Europe	Asia
	1990	1991	1992	1990	1991	1992	1992			
Automotive vehicles and parts	37.3	52.1	69.5	46.1	54.1	70.1	5.2	2.2	20.6	1.2
Telecommunications equipment	—	—	2.1	—	12.2	2.1	3.2	—	94.7	—
Foods and beverages	11.3	10.6	6.0	11.3	10.7	6.8	0.1	22.4	37.9	1.6
Total	16.2	21.0	28.8	17.9	21.6	29.5	2.0	15.1	32.0	1.4

Source: Calculated on the basis of data from authors' survey.

one food sector TE traditionally oriented toward exportation. Nevertheless, the export coefficient exhibited a downward trend for the period studied—a trend slightly reversed in 1993 and which perhaps will become upwardly oriented if the sampled manufacturing companies' current expectations are realized. This decline in the export coefficient was drastic in the case of the food manufacturing sector, but the automotive sector's export coefficient has actually been quite stable through 1992, with even a slight increase in 1993 (Table 2.17).

Argentina's structural reforms and overall macroeconomic situation (in the absence of sectoral regimens or product lines rigidly oriented toward exportation) have basically stimulated the surveyed manufacturing companies' imports and their sales on the domestic market. Their imports of finished goods have grown significantly—from 5 percent of total imports in 1990 to 36 percent in 1992. Meanwhile, imports of inputs have grown significantly, and capital goods inputs have remained low (Table 2.18).

These trends reflect the impact of trade liberalization and the higher level of related activity. In the case of finished goods, increased importation is often linked to the importing firms' complementation of their local production with imports of goods from the same company. These imports may be of certain company product lines still not produced in Argentina (usually at the upper end of the consumer scale or at the highest levels of technological sophistication), or the finished imports may be of products whose local production has been discontinued (whether because of intracorporative specialization programs, as in the automotive sector, or because of a decline in the profitability of certain production lines, such as in the telecommunications equipment sector).

The surveyed manufacturing firms' increased volume of imported inputs relates to their production increases and also to the lower degree of national integration of domestic processes. This decreased local participation in turn stems at least in part from the nature of the technological requirements of certain production lines, such as telecommunications.[36] It also stems in part from Argentina's trade liberalization. In the automotive sector, the fundamental factor has been the sectoral regimen's relaxation of local content requirements. Meanwhile, the continuing low level of capital goods imports (some of them consisting of used capital goods) probably indicates that the foreign investment process in the surveyed manufacturing sectors—at least in terms of production equipment imported by the firms themselves—had not, as of 1992, reached maximum levels.

The automobile industry's export performance is a consequence of the official sectoral regulatory regimen in effect since 1991. For producers, the regimen's

---

[36] Local telecommunications equipment production is of the CKD (completely knocked down) variety. The electronic components are imported, and the mechanical parts and assembly boards are manufactured in the local plant.

Table 2.17. Sample of Selected Firms: Export Coefficients, 1990–96 [a]
(Percentages)

Sector	1990	1991	1992	1993	Forecast of average annual coefficients 1994–96
Automotive vehicles and parts	10.4	10.2	10.1	13.3	21.7
Telecommunications equipment	0.1	5.1	2.5	3.1	3.1
Foods and beverages	74.3	53.5	48.2	49.5	49.1
Total	33.2	25.5	19.9	21.5	26.9

Source: Calculated on the basis of data from authors' survey.
[a] Calculated as the ratio between exports and production.

Table 2.18. Sample of Selected Firms: Composition of Imports, 1990–92
(Percentages)

Sector	Final Products			Inputs			Capital Goods		
	1990	1991	1992	1990	1991	1992	1990	1991	1992
Automotive vehicles and parts	0.2	21.1	35.1	95.2	1.56	63.2	4.6	17.4	1.7
Telecommunications equipment	25.4	34.5	43.0	71.0	61.5	49.2	3.6	4.0	7.8
Foods and beverages	37.7	30.2	41.1	56.5	54.3	50.1	5.8	15.5	8.8
Total	5.4	22.5	36.0	90.0	60.9	61.6	4.6	16.5	2.5

Source: Calculated on the basis of data from authors' surveys.

stimulus to production consisted of allowing them to keep their leadership position in the domestic auto market. Most analysts agree that if the Argentine market had been totally opened to vehicle imports, then local production of finished vehicles would have practically dried up or would have scaled back to simple assembly operations. In those circumstances a sizable chunk of the market currently covered by local producers would probably have been taken over by other producers—Asian, in particular.

Although most of the existing finished-vehicle producers in Argentina can access worldwide trading networks that could easily supply the Argentine market with finished vehicles produced at lower cost by their affiliates in other countries, they have found that the increased cost of producing locally has been offset by their enjoyment of a larger market share than they would have obtained had they supplied the market through imports. Moreover, two of the firms producing finished vehicles locally are controlled by Argentine nationals, who would have had no means of supplying the domestic market through intracompany imports—a fact that corroborates our interpretation of the official policy.

The sectoral regimen has not only helped the automotive sector to retain existing finished vehicle producers but has also sparked the return of a U.S. producer that had departed in the late 1970s, and has also stimulated interest on the part of several Japanese producers, who have announced plans for establishing plants in Argentina.

The new automotive sector regimen exacts a "price" from these producers in exchange for allowing them to maintain local production and participation in a domestic market enjoying rapidly rising consumer demand. Part of this "price" is the fact that their exports of finished vehicles and parts and pieces made in Argentina are in themselves not very profitable. The reduced marginal contribution by these exports is, however, counterbalanced by the higher prices commanded in the Argentine market by their locally produced units and by finished vehicle imports, which receive a more favorable tariff treatment than do similar imports by other agents in the economy. Clearly, though, high prices to consumers, as well as certain vehicle quality concerns, constitute problem areas of the official automotive regimen in terms of local consumers.

At this point it may be well for us to draw a distinction between exports of automotive parts and exports of finished vehicles. With respect to auto parts exports, at least one (and probably two) of the auto parts export projects invested in by the surveyed finished vehicle manufacturers had a level of profitability equal to or greater than the average profitability of the Argentine economy during the 1980s. But the increase in domestic costs in dollar terms has led to the present rate of return being lower than anticipated. Even so, these projects remain valuable components of the corporations' international and subregional operations, and one of the plants actually operates on an internationally competitive scale and uses highly competitive technology. The same scenario does not hold for exports of finished vehicles.

Most exports by the finished vehicle manufacturers consist of auto parts and pieces shipped to other affiliates of the same parent corporation, mostly within MERCOSUR. Nevertheless, because the sectoral regimen rewards the export of finished vehicles and because the levels of foreign exchange generated by auto parts exports do not cover the finished vehicle manufacturers' imports, in almost every case there now is (or is about to be) an "exclusive" assignment of a selected parent corporation auto model to be produced only by the local producer. Thus, exports of finished vehicles are expected to begin to attain higher volumes and greater profitability than they presently exhibit.

In this context, MERCOSUR has acquired great relevance for the automotive sector, in that the nature of the local affiliates' production specializations is defined largely vis-à-vis that of the Brazil-based affiliates. Beyond certain given demand preferences in the two countries (two-door cars in Brazil and four-door cars in Argentina), the general production specialization criterion will be that Argentine affiliates will produce some of the more sophisticated models, and Brazilian affiliates will produce the models that appeal more to the mass market. This decision is based on respective volumes of production: Argentina will have advantages (or, in the present context, fewer disadvantages, relatively speaking) in the manufacture of vehicle types for which the scale of production is less crucial for competitiveness.

It is important to note that in Argentina, MERCOSUR serves the automotive sector entirely through its specially administered trade regimen for the auto sector; in other words, the key feature for intermember trade is not the general program of tariff reductions but is instead the sectoral program governing automotive trade between Argentina and Brazil. In a hypothetical situation of total liberalization of regional trade, the Argentine auto affiliates would almost certainly respond in the manner described earlier to a unilateral opening to the rest of the world. Even if MERCOSUR is never fully implemented as an integration system, the crucial factor for the Argentine automotive sector would be the continuation of the special sectoral trade regimen.

Argentina's finished vehicle manufacturers thus plan to expand the finished vehicle component of their exports, largely destined for MERCOSUR, although in some cases significant exports to other regions are also being contemplated. Another route being explored to reduce their trade deficits is to develop local providers, especially in view of the change in the sectoral regime that stipulates that beginning in 1995 there must be a 60 percent national content integration, value-wise, into each individual model (not merely on the average for all models, as formerly allowed).

Up to this point, exports of auto parts and finished vehicles have increased markedly, but not all the official automotive regimen's stipulations have yet been complied with, nor have the MERCOSUR Protocol 21 quotas been filled. Apparently, it will be possible to remedy lags in Protocol 21 auto exports to Brazil, but it will be much more difficult to catch up with the shortfalls in export-related goals established by the sectoral regimen. In this regard, the Argentine government's relative passivity in ensuring compliance with the regimen underscores serious implementational difficulties that must be addressed.

Let us turn now to exports by the surveyed Argentine food and beverage manufacturers. The trade balance of these producers is strongly positive, but their import growth during the 1990s has been much more rapid than their export growth. We shall consider the sample's two strongly export-oriented food manufacturing companies separately from the other four surveyed food companies (even though the marketing strategies of the former are giving increasing importance to domestic sales). One of these two export-oriented companies operates primarily in the area of agricultural and agroindustrial commodities, such as grains and edible oils; the other manufactures cooked and canned meats, sold under U.S. and Western European corporate trademarks.[37] In addition to their export lines, both companies sell foods processed for Argentina's domestic market, where intercompany competition requires attention to such factors as brand name, packaging, advertising, and domination of distribution channels. These factors naturally are also crucial in the domestic marketing strategy of the other four manufacturers, which include one affiliate long established in the country, as well as three new foreign investors. These four companies produce dairy-based products, sweets, beverages, and other brand-name food items.

The logic behind locating in Argentina varies from company to company, and each company's position in the international marketing context is also different. For instance, for the two export-oriented companies, Argentina's abundance of food-related natural resources (and to a lesser degree Argentina's technological activities) constituted a catalyst for exporting from Argentina. On the other hand, these same two companies decided to use Argentina as a locale for domestically oriented food production—as did the four nonexport-oriented companies—largely because of Argentina's dual production and importation advantages, with the attendant availability of international and domestic marketing channels.

All of the food manufacturers test the domestic market with imported finished food items from the parent corporation, seeking out promising opportunities for local production. In general, the imported market test items come in small lots, not massive amounts; the test products that sell the best then become candidates for local production. The method is one that might be called an "import substitution" strategy.

---

[37] Because of food consumption preferences in Argentina, products such as these would not sell well on the domestic market, and so the firm necessarily has to export a large portion of its production.

The advantage of food manufacturing TEs (given a reasonable quality-to-price ratio in their local production) vis-à-vis food companies that only import stems largely from their management of the distribution channels. The advantage of food sector TE affiliates' over competing food manufacturing companies funded with local capital stems largely from their ability to combine different amounts of production, imports, and exports in accordance with the current activity level and relative-price structure, as well as from the benefits inherent in their access to intracompany marketing channels.

MERCOSUR currently does not have much relevance for this sector. Although most parent corporations with Argentine affiliates also have subsidiaries in Brazil, not much has been achieved thus far in terms of strategies for production complementation—a possibility envisioned more for the medium and long term. The parent company of the export-oriented producer of processed meats has no affiliate in Brazil, and thus the Brazilian market figures heavily in its medium-term export strategy.

The two telecommunications equipment producers have been oriented almost exclusively toward the domestic market. Through the late 1980s, within the country's closed market context, they enjoyed the privilege of being ENTEL's sole providers, with highly trained personnel and well-equipped plants. High returns from their operations resulted more from surcharges billed to a captive client than from any dynamic growth of demand.

The privatization of ENTEL and Argentina's economic liberalization process drastically altered this scenario, reducing the two producers' market shares as well as their domestic prices. Nevertheless, they continue to enjoy (in addition to a 10 percent price preference)[38] an advantage based on the fact that the country's existing telephone network is equipped with products manufactured by them. Imported equipment therefore has a certain penetration limit, because of the network's technological continuity requirements, which make it impractical for it to incorporate equipment from a new source into an existing telephone exchange.

---

[38] ENTEL's privatization specifications included an industrial policy clause granting a 10 percent preference to suppliers of installed telephone equipment in Argentina (the only such clause existing in any case of privatization in the country). But the two local providers of installed telephonic switching stations (or exchanges)—which currently account for roughly two-thirds of the lines acquired by ENTEL, with the remaining one-third supplied by foreign manufacturers—stated that the operators' criteria for selecting the winning bids have not been disclosed and that the competing suppliers' offers have not been made available for examination so that the local suppliers can verify if the 10 percent preference policy is being duly implemented. Furthermore, the corresponding regulatory body is not performing its established oversight function.

Even though tariff protection for telecommunications equipment producers is weak,[39] a growing demand and the perceived advantages of a local presence and firsthand knowledge of the market make local production a viable proposition, at least in the production of switching equipment. In addition to competing on the local market with imports, the two telecommunications equipment producers also have intracompany exports of high value-added services and goods to affiliates outside of Latin America. Even so, their slight export increase during the 1990s has not kept pace with their rapid increase in imports (of inputs as well as of finished goods), leading to a marked deterioration in the sector's trade balance.

Unlike the manufacturing firms, the sample's privatized enterprises are situated in the nontradables sector, with sales directed almost exclusively toward the domestic market.[40]

The privatization of public enterprises has produced a rise in imports of goods and services. Most of the surveyed privatized companies noted an increase in the participation of imports in the provision of equipment, inputs and materials, within the context of a general shift in the suppliers' structure. This shift has been facilitated by economic openness and by the expiration of rules on national content.

The implementation of the privatized sectors' investment plans had led to a notable increase in imports of machinery and equipment, which currently enter duty free. The most important development in this regard has been the entry of new suppliers of uninstalled telecommunications equipment with production plants located in Argentina.[41]

The increase in imports has not been limited to equipment but has included inputs as well. In addition, a significant foreign presence has been noted in construction works and equipment installation, often associated with the operators of the newly privatized enterprises. Except for the case of the privatized natural gas distribution enterprise, the arrival of the new foreign suppliers has not seemed to entail any transfers of know-how to local producers.

---

[39] Tariff rates on imported components are higher than the zero-level tariff rate governing imports of finished telecommunications equipment, but even so, the importing companies receive (if only temporarily) from the government a 15 percent reimbursement (which has, however, been somewhat difficult to collect).

[40] The telephone companies receive payments from abroad for international calls and data transmission services. It is also conceivable that other privatized public service companies could likewise begin to generate exports. For instance, electric power suppliers could perhaps export energy to neighboring countries, or gas and electric energy transporters could also export their services. But thus far, no such additional export experiences have materialized.

[41] Two of the new suppliers have the same country of origin as two of the foreign operators of the privatized phone companies, and one of them is in fact an affiliate of one of the operators—a suggestive state of affairs in a sector in which there exist few bidders at the international level and in which the associated world trade has certain features in common with "administered" trade.

Within a framework of lowered tariff protection, the increased penetration by imports seems to be related primarily to lower prices (telephone equipment), higher quality, or lack of availability of local supply (generation and distribution of electricity, transport of natural gas). The availability of new suppliers with "easy" finance terms has induced significant price cuts by local producers of telephone equipment.[42] On the other hand, the privatized public service enterprises' cost for obtaining civil engineering works does not seem any lower than before. Because many providers of civil engineering works appear to be associated (even corporately) with the privatized companies' technical operators or their partners, it is possible that there may be occurring a hidden transfer of profits by means of the payment of inflated charges. This same maneuver could also be serving to "inflate" the privatized companies' investment costs in fulfillment of the investment expenditure requirements stipulated in the bid specifications of the different privatizations (water, natural gas and telephone services). In any case, one of the purposes of the respective regulatory bodies—which have different operational modes and schedules in each case—is to be on the alert for this type of behavior.

Technological and Organizational Contributions

Management, Productivity and Quality

Privatization led to drastic management-related changes in public service enterprises. The present managers have embarked upon development of a new organizational culture, applying modern management techniques at all levels and massively incorporating computer-based equipment and routines and modern administrative systems. Activities related to input purchases and subcontracting have also been changed to reduce costs and shorten delivery time. In the distribution enterprises, one of the new management's main objectives is to increase company income through improved client registration and better management of collection-related activities.

Not many indicators are available, but labor productivity seems to have increased in privatized enterprises as a result of initial staff cuts and new management techniques. In some cases, these changes have led to improved quality of services.

In telecommunications, the ratio between the number of phone lines in service and the number of employees dramatically increased between 1990 and 1993,

---

[42] Domestic prices have gone down by half, to $200 per line. The winning bid on a recent phone company contract was made by a supplier linked to one of that phone company's foreign operators, at a price of $150 per line, notwithstanding local providers' complaints of dumping.

even as service quality also began to improve (surpassing the goals established in the bid specifications) and new services began to be made available, particularly in 1993 (Table 2.19). Even so, the phone companies' improved indicators of productivity and service density still fall far short of the counterpart indicators recorded in other countries served by the foreign operators' parent corporations.[43] The service quality gap compared to other countries also remains wide, and there still exists a wide difference in rates.[44]

With respect to natural gas services, the regulatory body has already imposed more than $1 million worth of fines on transporters and distributors, usually for supply-related problems (service interruptions or lack of gas pressure) and billing errors. In the opinion of the interviewed gas distribution enterprise, service quality is "horrible" and the gap with the parent company will not soon be closed. With respect to water services, six months of operation have brought consumers some service improvements (Table 2.20). With respect to fuel burning electrical generating stations, a relatively longer period of operation has brought consumers an appreciably enhanced availability of electricity (Table 2.21).

In electricity distribution enterprises, exploitation expenditures have declined, as has the length of service interruptions following weather-related outages, but the most complex problem remains that of power theft, and inroads against it have been less effective than desired (Table 2.21). The regulatory body has imposed more than $9 million worth of fines on both electricity distributors for failing to meet the earlier-established quality standards. In addition, heavy investments (as yet not forthcoming from the enterprises) will be needed to reduce the current 10 percent level of technical power loss by half, thereby meeting international standards.

It is difficult to pinpoint foreign partners' precise contribution to technical and organizational improvements. There does exist a clear distinction between the case of telecommunications services, which in recent years have experienced a tremendous technological leap forward, and the case of the other privatized enterprises, in which the pace of available technical changes is slow. In the first

---

[43] In France, Italy and Spain, the number of lines in service per 100 residents is 48, 42 and 35 respectively, and the number of lines in service per phone company employee is 198, 257 and 194.

[44] In this regard, Coloma et al. (1992, p. 271) state that "the rapid deterioration of phone operations that occurred in 1989 and 1990 worked in favor of Telefónica's and Telecom's fulfillment of their objectives, allowing them to achieve relatively rapid improvements by simply reestablishing prior levels of quality and by repairing the many installed but out-of-service lines left to them by the state-run company." Urban telephone rates in Argentina are now similar to urban rates in the United States, but intercity rates are eight times higher, and international rates are three and one-half times higher, according to data from the regulatory body. Line installation rates are also higher in Argentina than in the United States, even though they have decreased appreciably since privatization of the phone service.

Table 2.19. Indicators of Telephone Companies' Quality and Productivity, 1990–93

	1990		1992		1993				Goals	
	Company A	Company B	Company A	Company B	Company A	Mandatory objectives	Company B	Mandatory objectives	Company A	Company B
Lines installed	1,915,000	1,556,000	2,258,000	1,999,000	2,666,000	2,249,000	2,301,000	1,841,000	4,028,000	2,910,000
Users receiving service	1,695,000	1,391,000	1,008,000	1,674,000	2,213,000	n.a.	1,878,000	n.a.	3,474,000	n.a.
Public telephones installed	12,749	9,800	20,686	15,814	24,027	18,759	20,524	15,057	39,000	n.a.
Lines in service/employee	78	73	104	98	122	n.a.	120	n.a.	186	187
Lines in service/100 inhabitants	12	11	13	10	14	n.a.	11	n.a.	20	14
Digitalization of network (%)	15	12	24	32	38	n.a.	54	n.a.	72	86
Average repair time (days)	8	15	24	n.a.	737	n.a.	n.a.	n.a.	n.a.	n.a.
Waiting time for hookup (months)	n.a.	n.a.	n.a	12	n.a.	12	7	12	n.a.	n.a.
Lines out of service (%)	5	7	—	1	—	n.a.	—	n.a.	n.a.	n.a.
Pending breakdowns	90,259	n.a.	4,111	n.a.	3,965	n.a.	n.a.	n.a.	n.a.	n.a.

Sources: Company reports, Gerchunoff and Cánovas (1993) and FIEL (1992).

Table 2.20. Indicators of Quality of Water Services, 1993

	May 1, 1993	November 1, 1993
Water pipe leakages needing attention	2,000	500
Average age of work order (days)	90	2
Sewerage blockages needing attention	3,000	1,500

Source: Company reports.

Table 2.21. Indicators of Quality and Productivity of Electric Services, 1991–93

Generator Stations	May 31, 1991	November 30, 1992
Availability (%)	43.0	75
Agents per megawatt	1.0	0.5
Distributor Station	September 30, 1992	December 31, 1943
Energy loss (%)		
- Company A	30.0	27
- Company B	26.0	23
Production costs per megawatt hour sold ($)		
- Company A	29.1	23
Service interruption time per month (hrs.)		
- Company B	2.3	1.1
Power provided to users (megawatts per month)		
- Company B	1,696	1,860
Technical capacity for responding to service and information requests (monthly communication units)		
- Company B	22,000	82,000

Sources: Gerchunoff and Cánovas (1993), and company data.

case, no one would dispute the important impact of foreign operators in facilitating the rapid dissemination of available new telecommunications technologies, primarily through the participation of experienced new foreign personnel. In the other sectors, in the absence of significant technological innovations, foreign operators have instead focused their efforts upon task automatization and efficiency enhancement.

Some might maintain that the "FDI" effect has not really been as strong as the "privatization" effect in improving the performance of the privatized public service enterprises. It might well be that in many cases the application of business criteria different from those prevalent during state management of these enterprises has been the primary force behind productivity and management improvements and cost reductions. The demands of the regulatory bodies and the requirements imposed by the privatization bid specs have been in many cases the catalysts behind quality improvements, and in many other cases these quality improvements have been motivated primarily by the privatized enterprises' desire to achieve greater profitability.

Although for certain privatized enterprises the "reputation" factor alone may possibly have provided sufficient incentive for raising the quality of services provided to users,[45] certain standards established in the privatization bid specs would almost certainly not have been observed with the same intensity and alacrity by the enterprises if these standards had not been clearly spelled out—a perception corroborated by the number of fines that have had to be imposed by the regulatory bodies.

The principal foreign contribution (mainly in the natural gas and electric power sectors) would seem to reside in the actual organization of the new firm and in the new business created by the privatization.[46] The FDI contribution could reside in the creation of new business structures in what had formerly been a section of a state enterprise. This new business segmentation has also entailed the implementation of new types of mercantile transactions such as charging a toll for the transmission of electricity or natural gas. The foreign firms, familiar with the functioning of these types of operations, contribute their experience in the management of new purchasing and sales functions earlier untried in the country.

There have also been changes in manufacturing firms (although less intensive than in the privatized enterprises) to bring about substantial improvements in these firms' administration and production management and to reduce affiliates' productivity gaps and quality gaps vis-à-vis their parent TEs.

In a context in which most of the firms operating in Argentina in the tradables sectors have implemented streamlining strategies aimed at achieving cost reductions and improvements in operational efficiency, the surveyed manufacturing firms have been no exception to the rule. In addition, they have seen their prod-

---

[45] It could be argued that this element of "reputation" would be more relevant in the case of foreign investors, given the greater scope—geographically and in terms of time span—of their involvement in the sector.

[46] The state-owned natural gas company, *Gas del Estado,* formerly had a monopoly on the transport and distribution of gas, and the state-owned petroleum company, YPF, had a monopoly on production. The privatization of some of YPF's oil and gas reserves allowed new producers to enter the market. Later, upon the privatization of *Gas del Estado,* gas transport and distribution adopted an unintegrated operational structure comprising two natural gas transporters and eight distributors. In the electricity sector, although formerly there had already existed more than one operator in the areas of power generation, transmission and distribution, all three areas had been encompassed by the large companies. As in the natural gas sector, privatization led to the segmentation of these larger companies, which were divided into generation, transmission and distribution firms.

uct lines benefit from a domestic demand increase greater than the demand increase affecting the products of the average Argentine industrial firm.

Among the sampled producers of finished vehicles, physical productivity increased by around 160 percent between 1990 and 1993 (from 6.8 to 17.5 vehicles per employee); in terms of the number of worker hours required as input into the manufacture of a single vehicle, there occurred a 20 percent to 25 percent improvement during that same period. Despite the improvement since 1990 (the worst year in the history of that particular branch of industry in Argentina) and despite the improvement in comparison with the branch's entire past in the Argentine economy, these levels are still much lower than international levels.[47] Furthermore, the customary quality concerns were probably aggravated by the hefty increase in production volume. The new manufacturing techniques being explored by the surveyed firms in conjunction with their suppliers should introduce substantial improvements in quality assurance.

Despite the reduction in the levels of domestic content required in their products, the manufacturers seem interested in developing their network of suppliers in order to reduce their degree of vertical integration, which exceeds international best-practice standards. To satisfy increasingly stringent quality and price requirements, these manufacturers and the large producers of auto parts are facilitating the adaptation process through the acquisition of technical assistance, and they are seeking to join with Brazilian firms in an effort toward technological updating and specialization. In addition, the development of suppliers is designed to help satisfy the regimen's requirements in regard to each firm's trade balance.

The process of incorporating new manufacturing techniques is proceeding unevenly in the sector. On the one hand, there is the newly arrived producer whose plans include the application of key elements of "lean production" (Womack et al., 1990) and other practices similar to those used in its larger U.S. plants, with the help of recently recruited personnel under a specially negotiated collective labor contract and in a specially refurbished assembly plant.

On the other hand, in the rest of the finished vehicle firms in Argentina, the adoption of new techniques is still at an embryonic stage and is occurring in a rather scattered way. Within a context of rapid growth of the number of finished

---

[47] Although comparison is hampered by various differences (in degree of vertical integration, fabrication techniques, level of automation, and economies of scale), it is nonetheless useful to note that the per-vehicle time of the "best-practice" assembly operation in Japan, the United States and Europe was 13.2, 18.6 and 22.7 hours respectively (Womack, Jones and Roos, 1990), with a comparable estimated figure of 35 to 45 hours per vehicle as assembled in Argentine auto plants. Current worker productivity in auto factories in Japan is around 80 vehicles per worker, and in Europe the current figure is approximately 45 vehicles per worker (*The Economist*, Feb. 5, 1994).

units produced, such a radical change in the conception of manufacturing methods as is implied by the new techniques is hindered by sunken costs in the manufacturing equipment, the assembly line tradition of local production, suppliers' uneven level of technological development, and the entrenched routine of line workers and supervisors.

One of the auto parts manufacturers associated with a finished vehicle producer (the recently opened transmission factory described earlier) displays a high degree of automatization, with production work organized into various work stations in which highly trained operators are responsible for process quality. The other parts producers have also introduced new manufacturing techniques (based on layout changes, team labor, and drastic stock reductions) that have helped to improve productivity and quality indicators, even though there remain wide gaps in these areas compared with their parent corporations.

With respect to telecommunications equipment, product quality is comparable to that achieved in the countries of origin of the associated technology. In recent years, to compensate for the price drop, productivity has increased significantly, largely through changes in organizational structures and in production logistics, including greater efforts and higher requirements in the development of local suppliers. Differences in production functions between local and foreign plants hampers a precise comparison of productivity, but it is clear that the scale of operations works against Argentine establishments.

Among the food and beverage manufacturers, maintenance of product quality is not a serious problem. Nevertheless, the penetration of the Argentine market by imported items has prompted local producers to improve their products' packaging, presentation, distribution and advertising. In the more export-oriented firms, recent productivity growth has been the result of improvements in organization and production; in the nonexport-oriented firms, productivity growth has been mainly the result of improvements in distribution. The company in which the greatest efforts toward quality assurance have been required has been the processed meat producer, which, in order to comply with industrialized country import standards, particularly in regard to measures against hoof-and-mouth disease, has had to implement (among other things) a thoroughgoing quality control system.

The type of contribution made by FDI in the surveyed food manufacturing firms varies widely according to the sectors involved. The introduction of new products generally depends on technology contributed by the parent company. Foreign investors' input into food marketing and packaging is also crucial. In some cases, the foreign investors have also helped to establish quality standards. On the other hand, different firms exhibit different levels of foreign input into the areas of organizational innovation and process technology. In some cases the local affiliates appear to function in these areas relatively autonomously and to be the initiators of any changes made, but in other cases the local affiliates, especially the relatively new ones, receive a good deal of input into these areas from the parent company.

Personnel Training

One of the elements frequently cited as a potential competitive advantage for Argentina in projects based on international specialization—namely, the availability of qualified labor at a relatively low cost—was not mentioned by the surveyed FDI firms as being a motivating factor behind any of their export strategies. In fact, these firms stated that the labor factor actually had a negative impact in terms of costs (as a result of currency appreciation) and even of quality (somewhat surprisingly).

In the view of some of the interviewed companies, especially in the automotive and auto parts sectors, the quality and qualifications of local assembly line workers have declined over the years. These companies point out, for instance, their difficulty in finding qualified metalworkers in the local labor market—a situation that has forced them to carry out their recent personnel increases by hiring less qualified labor and then providing the new workers with ad hoc training activities. Training costs in industry have in fact been highest in the automotive and auto parts sectors. The same scenario has also prevailed, on a smaller scale, in the sector that manufactures telecommunications equipment.[48]

Generally, the manufacturers of finished vehicles have their own technical schools. In addition, they have adopted, in cooperation with Argentine educational authorities, a dual factory-based and classroom-based training plan for workers beginning at 15 years of age, and they have also developed, in cooperation with the Ministry of Labor, a six-month in-class and in-plant training program for workers displaced from other sectors to facilitate their entry into the automotive sector.

In addition, on-the-job training for workers, supervisors and administrative personnel is crucial, as are special courses for middle and upper management. In some cases, staff members are sent to the parent company (especially in the Brazilian affiliates) for training, but most training is provided by local company staff and specialized consultants.

All of the surveyed firms stressed the importance of training, but the new Brazilian managers of an auto parts factory seem to be the ones who are making

---

[48] The surveyed companies did not present data on the monetary value of their training expenditures—in most cases simply because they do not have any such data. The exception was a telecommunications equipment manufacturer that spends approximately 0.8 percent of the value of its sales on training activities. Given the generalized lack of training expenditure data from other Argentine manufacturers, however, it has not been possible to effect any intercompany comparison in this area.

the greatest effort to modify worker habits through training. In any case, the most ambitious training plans of all are those of the new finished vehicle plant relocating in Argentina.

In the surveyed set of manufacturing firms, the number of foreigners on staff is quite low and is concentrated in the "newcomer" firms. Among the privatized enterprises, only in exceptional cases did managers from the former state-run companies retain their high-level jobs after privatization. The foreign operators have brought to Argentina some 350 technicians and executives who work in the new firms (160 in telecommunications services and 100 in electric power distribution), in addition to temporary staff brought in to provide technical assistance. The remainder of the executive positions have been filled primarily by specialists recruited in the employment market and by personnel from local operational partners and, to a lesser degree, from international banks.

The new operators have stated that their largest personnel-related problems stem from overstaffing, corruption on the part of some agents, uneven technical preparation of inherited personnel, and poor work habits carried over from the state enterprises. In order to change this situation, great emphasis has been placed upon personnel training, and modern management techniques are being introduced. In addition, the changes that have been introduced should lead to increases in the relative number of technicians and professionals within the employment structures.[49] Consonant with their rapidly increasing technological requirements, the telephone service enterprises are the firms with the most expenditures earmarked for training. The electricity, natural gas and water service companies have also begun to provide training courses for their personnel, and they plan to increase this type of activities, although to varying degrees.

In the case of the telephone service enterprises, training basically covers the management of new technologies and is oriented primarily toward personnel working in outside facilities. In the electric power enterprises and especially in the natural gas enterprises, training covers the new marketing approaches that were introduced with privatization. In both cases, these marketing-related training tasks are carried out primarily by temporary foreign personnel. Other training tasks are performed largely by local instructors, and the contribution of foreign partners is limited to very specific technologies related to the operation of the business.

---

[49] One of the privatized telephone companies does not recruit workers without high school diplomas and has incorporated many professionals into its staff (professionals constituted 1.8 percent of total employees in 1990 and 7.5 percent by 1993). In one fuel burning electrical power station, the ratio of professionals to the total number of employees increased from 8 percent to 16 percent.

Research and Development Activities

In contrast to the high intensity of the firms' activities targeted at improving quality and productivity, their research and development (R&D) and engineering activities have thus far been of very limited scope. Among the privatized enterprises, only one of the phone service companies has a R&D laboratory. This lab has a staff of 70 engineers, and its developmental tasks are related to specific operational problems facing the firm in Argentina. The work is performed independently of the parent corporation's own R&D activities.

Within the manufacturing sector, the greatest concentration of R&D resources has been found among the telecommunications equipment manufacturers. One has allocated 150 employees and 3 percent of its sales receipts to R&D, and the other has approximately 30 persons working in product development to take advantage of market niches (low-capacity switching stations, some electronic components, and certain types of software). One firm even granted licenses to the parent corporation for manufacturing and marketing its products in other affiliates, and it has also arranged for some exports.

In the food manufacturing sector, the two export-oriented firms are also the firms that are the most actively oriented toward research and development. One of the firms is performing R&D related to seed development and has 50 persons working in that area; the other firm has a pilot plant and a staff of 10 technicians for the development of new products. In the automotive sector, R&D activities have focused primarily upon adapting parent company models or Brazilian affiliate models to Argentine conditions, for which the finished vehicle manufacturers have small R&D technical and engineering staffs.

Conclusions and Policy Recommendations

Lessons from the Argentine Experience

Clearly, there are generic reasons that frame and help explain the behavior of the new FDI in Argentina. Beyond the international factors (a dimension not covered in the present study), the level of country risk was reduced by the renegotiation of the foreign debt and the application of a broad program of structural reforms. The resultant stability and revitalization of the Argentine economy were decisive catalysts for transnational enterprises' investment decisions. Interestingly, changes in specific aspects of FDI regulations did not appear to have been significant elements of attraction for FDI.

This favorable overall economic framework, however, does not explain either the magnitude or the sectoral distribution of recent FDI. These two FDI aspects appear to have been determined by very specific policies and

sider that there are significant official expectations regarding future FDI inflows in terms of their potential positive impact both upon the financing needs associated with the country's external imbalance and upon the aim of increasing the economy's productivity level. The income foreseen from the remaining privatizable public enterprises does not amount to very much, and no huge expansion is foreseen of the market opportunities that have up to this point attracted spontaneous inflows of FDI.

Meanwhile, although the recent FDI inflows have generated positive externalities for the economy as a whole, the market-guided investments registered thus far in the tradables sectors have no explicit export-oriented strategies (these investments are concentrated in the food manufacturing sector and consist largely of purchases of already-existing firms). Furthermore, there does not yet appear to be any important technological spillovers from the new FDI.

These trends suggest the need to implement specific new policies to ensure not only quantity but also quality in the incorporation of FDI. Thus, the issues at hand become the factual design of these instruments and the nature of the actions and goals to be defined and regulated. Their conceptualization and especially their implementation should comprise mechanisms to ensure a quid pro quo arrangement based on official requirements for the FDI's creation of positive externalities. The effectiveness of these active and selective policies will undoubtedly depend upon a satisfactory negotiation of goals and performance requirements and upon the will and capacity to exercise the power of control.[53]

It is important to remember that beginning with the setting of the nominal exchange rate under the Convertibility Plan, the Argentine economy has evolved along a relative-price pathway that penalizes the country's tradables sectors. In addition, the country's process of opening up its domestic market occurred within a context of a historically overvalued national currency. In such a framework, the reactivation of domestic demand that followed the stabilization shock exerted strong pressure on the economy's external sector, and Argentina's trade deficit has steadily climbed since 1992.

The industrial policy definitions (based largely upon marketing-oriented mechanisms) that began to be made at that time, and which naturally have had an impact on FDI's performance, have been governed fundamentally by the problem of the current account deficit and, more generally, by the problem of the exchange rate. Beyond the broad-scope actions adopted to improve the effective export exchange rate and raise the cost of bringing in imports, specific sectoral measures have been implemented that restrict certain imports or make them profitable in the short term. The postponement of the applicable sanctions in the case

---

[53] In reality, not only the TEs but also companies funded by domestic capital should be subject to these policies.

of the finished vehicle producers' noncompliance with their official exportation requirements could be explained by these factors.

Thus, the industrial policy does not seem to form a well-articulated whole, but instead consists of a loose patchwork of partial solutions to a problem that is essentially macroeconomic in origin. Furthermore, the type of incentives upon which this industrial policy is based does not necessarily promote improvements in the "quality" of the investment and overlooks certain potential positive externalities. This point should be carefully taken into account in the definition of an FDI policy.

The recent arrival of TEs that dominate the international processed-food marketing networks could constitute a good point of departure for negotiating commitments on exports and technological contributions. Within the framework of a local economy open to international competition, the decision of these TEs to manufacture certain products locally reflects genuine competitiveness. The development of new exports could be based upon this attribute of competitiveness and upon the new corporations' international distribution networks. If the resultant export or technology transfer commitments imply some type of official fiscal, credit or tariff incentive, the incentive should be granted only on a temporary basis and only as a function of specific counterconcessions, subject to verification and to fines if not forthcoming.

In this way, for instance, FDI could help Argentina participate in a two-way globalization process—that is, not only as an attractive market but also as an exporter of value-added goods and services, as is happening in the automotive sector.

In addition, Argentina should make use of the exceptional opportunity presented by the automotive sector's current unprecedented stage of outward development to initiate an automotive sector industrial policy within MERCOSUR that would induce finished vehicle producers to carry out greater technological efforts in the plants themselves. These firms should also be motivated to become more committed to strengthening the productive and managerial capacity of local auto parts producers, in order to reduce the large lag vis-à-vis international best practice, thereby making possible the gradual programmed reduction of protection levels on local production.

With respect to the performance of the privatized enterprises, the high-priority recommendation for public policy is that it ensure that all of the regulatory and controlling bodies carry out the tasks assigned them with regard to price regulation, service quality and investment commitments. In this sense the aspect that must be most promptly addressed in the telecommunications service sector is the high intercity and international charges. In the natural gas, water service and electric power sectors, the most pressing issues are service quality and compliance with investment programs.

Only one of these privatized enterprises has a research and development staff, but all of these enterprises have plans for substantially improving the technologies they utilize and for providing personnel training. It would be advisable to try to coordinate these efforts in order to increase the scarce resources assigned to such tasks in Argentina.

While keeping in mind the need to be alert to possible collusion between privatized firms and local or foreign suppliers associated with the consortia (which should be looked into by the regulatory bodies to prevent possible overbilling or underbilling that would affect the declared levels of profit and investment), the equipment purchases that the privatized enterprises are making or are planning to make could well have a favorable effect upon the local capital goods industry. The fact that local suppliers of telecommunications equipment have been able to maintain a majority participation in the market (while reducing prices, expanding production, and even carrying out export and R&D activities) suggests the potential of similar situations in other areas of the industry.

In any case, the local capital goods industry is faced with the negative effects of weak tariff protection and scarcity of long-term financing, and it will need more support than that provided by simple locational advantages and by prospects of increased demand for its products. The development of competitive capacity in the capital goods sector calls for a specific official policy that will link the privatized enterprises' investment plans and supply policies, possibilities of technology updating installed capacity, export promotion mechanisms, and Argentina's commitments to negotiating a common external tariff under MERCOSUR.

Argentina's generalized trade liberalization and the influx of new investors should, in theory, increase competition in the domestic markets for goods and services; the present restructuring of the country's economy (within which the new FDI is occurring) is, however, leading to a strong concentration of ownership by only a few. In view of this situation, Argentina must absolutely have at its disposal the necessary legal instruments for preventing monopolistic practices and the abuse of dominant positions.

In this regard, since existing legislation (Law 22.262 of 1980) that defends competition is inadequate to the task of addressing the problems presented by the new economic context, various bills are under discussion in Parliament (including a bill presented in 1992 by the government's executive branch). This legislative process needs to be accelerated so that a specific law defending competition can be passed as soon as possible. This new law should not only define the various prohibited monopolistic or collusive practices but should also provide the government with the proper technical bodies for adequately investigating and punishing abuses.

In summary, the principal lesson to be derived from the case of Argentina is that most of the increasing inflows of foreign direct investment have been attracted by specific policies. Nevertheless, these policy instruments would hardly have been as effective (and additional inflows of market-guided FDI would not have materialized) if inflation had not suddenly tapered off and if domestic demand had not grown steadily.

Those instruments tend to dwindle in effectiveness as factors that attract FDI. Furthermore, they were not originally designed to maximize FDI's potential contribution to economic development. This suggests the need to reformulate the scope and content of these policy instruments. Within the favorable context created by the reduction of the country risk, the new policy instruments should provide for the establishment of FDI performance goals in order to achieve a higher quality of incoming investment and should also incorporate effective mechanisms for ensuring the achievement of these goals.

Bibliography

Aspiazu, D. 1992. Las empresas transnacionales en una economía en transición: la experiencia argentina en los años ochenta. Paper presented at the Simposio de Alto Nivel sobre la Contribución de las Empresas Transnacionales al Crecimiento y el Desarrollo de América Latina y el Caribe, Santiago.

Bisang, R., and B. Kosacoff. 1993. Las exportaciones industriales en una economía en transformación: las sorpresas del caso argentino, 1974–1990. In *El desafío de la competitividad. La industria argentina en transición*, ed. B. Kosacoff. Buenos Aires: ECLAC/Alianza.

Coloma, G., P. Gerchunoff, and M.R. Schiacapasse. 1992. Empresa Nacional de Telecomunicaciones (ENTEL). In *Las privatizaciones en la Argentina. Primera etapa*, ed. P. Gerchunoff. Buenos Aires: Instituto Torcuato di Tella.

Economic Commission for Latin America and the Caribbean (ECLAC). 1992. *Inversión extranjera directa en América Latina y el Caribe, 1970–1990*. Santiago: ECLAC.

Fanelli, J.M., and M. Damill. 1993. Los capitales externos en las economías latinoamericanas: Argentina. In *Los capitales extranjeros en las economías latinoamericanas*, ed. J.A. Ocampo. Bogota: Inter-American Development Bank and FEDESARROLLO.

Fundación de Investigaciones Económicas Latinoamericanas (FIEL). 1992. *Capital de infraestructura en la Argentina. Gestión pública, privatización y productividad*. Buenos Aires: FIEL.

Fuchs, M. 1990. *Los programas de capitalización de la deuda externa argentina*. Buenos Aires: ECLAC.

Gerchunoff, P., and G. Canovas. 1993. Las privatizaciones en la Argentina: impactos micro y macroeconómicos. Buenos Aires. Mimeo.

Katz, J., and B. Kosacoff. 1989. *El proceso de industrialización en la Argentina: evolución, retroceso y prospectiva*. Buenos Aires: Centro Editor de América Latina (CEAL).

Kosacoff, B., and G. Bezchinsky. 1993. De la sustitución de importaciones a la globalización. Las empresas transnacionales en la industria argentina. In *El desafío de la competitividad. La industria argentina en transición*, editor B. Kosacoff. Buenos Aires: ECLAC/Alianza.

Ministerio de Economía. 1993. *Argentina en crecimiento.* Buenos Aires: Ministerio de Economía.

Sourrouille, J., J. Lucangeli, and B. Kosacoff. 1985. *Transnacionalización y política económica en la Argentina.* Buenos Aires: Centro de Economía Transnacional (CET)-CEAL.

Todesca, J. 1992. Competitividad del sector automovilístico argentino. Secretaría de Programación Económica/Subsecretaría de Estudios Económicos, Buenos Aires.

Vispo, A., and B. Kosacoff. 1991. *Difusión de tecnologías de punta en la Argentina: algunas reflexiones sobre la organización industrial de IBM.* Working Paper No. 38. ECLAC, Buenos Aires.

Womack, J.P., D.T. Jones, and D. Roos. 1990. *The Machine that Changed the World.* New York: Rawson - McMillan.

CHAPTER THREE

FOREIGN DIRECT INVESTMENT IN CHILE, 1987–93: UTILIZATION OF COMPARATIVE ADVANTAGES AND DEBT CONVERSION*

Luis Riveros
Jaime Vatter
Manuel R. Agosin

The economic process experienced by Chile during recent decades has been characterized by growing internationalization. During the early stages (1974–79), a thorough trade liberalization was implemented, followed by the opening up of the economy's capital account (1977–81). Within this strategy, foreign direct investment (FDI) had the fundamental role of providing the necessary capital for the development process as well as supplying the necessary technology and market knowledge for achieving export diversification in terms of both markets and products. As a function of these objectives, appropriate legal mechanisms on FDI were devised—most importantly, Decree Law 600 (DL 600), promulgated in 1974. Even so, FDI in Chile only began to increase significantly in 1987. Between 1974 and 1985, the value of FDI projects amounted to $2.364 billion, or roughly $200 million per year. Although this base figure may now appear small, it should be viewed within the economic context of the period. For instance, during the 1975–85 period, Chile's average annual exports were on the order of $3.254 billion—only one-third of what they are today. On the average, then, the value of FDI during that period amounted to 6 percent of the value of exports. In 1993, the value of FDI entering Chile through the provisions of DL 600 amounted to roughly 16 percent of the value of exports. These figures indicate that FDI was already significant in relation to other economic aggregates during the late 1970s and early 1980s. They also underscore FDI's growing importance, in both absolute and relative terms.

*The authors of the present chapter gratefully acknowledge the collaboration of Luis Figueroa and Christian Fresard, as well as that of José Luis Cuevas, who assisted in the survey. Thanks also to Daniel Chudnovsky, Jorge Sapoznikow and Roberto Steiner for their helpful comments.

Chile not only used the standard DL 600 mechanism but also made good use of the period in which Chilean foreign debt titles were being offered on the world market at prices considerably lower than their face value. It was in this context that in 1985 the country instituted a debt conversion program for nationals residing outside of the country who might wish to invest in Chile. This new mechanism (called "Chapter XIX") brought about a significant increase in FDI inflows, as well as an important reduction of Chile's external debt and the attendant interest payments. It included certain discretionary policy measures regarding the approval of investments (on a case-by-case basis), in contrast to DL 600, which essentially granted (nearly) automatic approval. One aspect that has aroused a certain degree of controversy is that Chapter XIX implied significant subsidies to investors—subsidies that could theoretically have been responsible for creating some substitution between FDI inflows through DL 600 and FDI inflows through Chapter XIX (Desormeaux, 1989; Ffrench-Davis, 1990).

This chapter seeks to determine the causes of the significant rise in FDI inflows into Chile beginning in 1987 and to define the impact that this has had upon that country's development process. We shall try to determine if Chapter XIX was a decisive factor in fostering the FDI increase during this mechanism's period of full applicability (1986–90), and we shall examine the relevance of FDI laws as well as certain elements of economic policy that have been especially important. In addition, we shall analyze FDI's impact on capital assets formation, export growth and diversification (by market and by product), and technology transfer—all of which are elements of great importance to Chile's current economic growth process.

The first section analyzes Chilean laws on FDI and describes the evolution of FDI in terms of the different existing mechanisms as well as in sectoral terms. The second section focuses on determining the causes of the FDI upswing observed since 1987; an econometric model is utilized in the quantitative analysis, and a qualitative analysis is based on a special survey of foreign investors. The third section examines the contribution of FDI to Chilean development through its impact on investment, exports and technological progress. An econometric model is utilized to study FDI's impact on investment, while the survey approach is used to address other areas of interest. The fourth section presents the conclusions and policy lessons drawn from the Chilean experience.

FDI Inflows and Their Regulation

Institutional Aspects and FDI Regulations

In recent years there have been two legal frameworks in Chile regulating FDI—namely, Decree Law 600 (DL 600) and Chapter XIX of the Compendium of

International Exchange Regulations of the Central Bank of Chile.[1] In effect since 1974, DL 600 deals largely with FDI made by foreign investors seeking assurances of national treatment and guarantees of the right to repatriate their capital and to remit profits abroad. Chapter XIX, which was implemented in 1985 and remained in effect until 1990, dealt largely with foreign investments carried out through the use of Chilean external debt titles.

The objectives of Chapter XIX were not only to promote FDI but also to reduce the burden of foreign debt. Accordingly, this mechanism had a great impact during the 1986–90 period both upon total FDI and upon the successful reduction of the country's total foreign obligations. Beginning in 1991, Chapter XIX declined in importance, and at present, DL 600 is the only legal instrument used, in practice, to carry out FDI in Chile.

Within the institutional framework, we should also mention the role played by the Foreign Investment Committee. The purposes of this institution are to analyze, authorize and promote FDI, and to gather investment-related information. In reality, the Foreign Investment Committee is the executive arm of DL 600. This decree law is a simple regulation that grants the covered foreign investors certain privileges and also places upon them certain minimum requirements. The latter consist of time terms on actually carrying out the capital investment, obligatory minimum time terms on the duration of the invested capital's stay in Chile (recently reduced to one year), and the investing company's presentation of certain basic qualifying background data. The privileges that DL 600 grants to investors include nearly unrestricted access to the domestic market (although the government reserves certain strategic sectors such as defense and nuclear energy), national treatment, tariff and value-added tax invariability for the entire investment period, unrestricted access to the formal exchange market in order to remit profits or eventually to repatriate capital, and the choice between a 10-year period of tax invariability or the national income tax regimen.[2] Profits may be remitted immediately and no taxes are applied. Industrial or extractive investment projects (including mining projects) that exceed $50 million in value may extend their tax invariability period to 20 years, carry out their accounting procedures in dollars, and contractually define their depreciation regimens and other accounting-related concepts—all of which help provide greater legal and institutional stability for this type of project. Export-oriented investment projects that exceed $50 million in value have additional benefits related to enhanced flexibility for returning foreign exchange.

---

[1] FDI can also be brought in directly by means of Chapter XIV of the Central Bank's Compendium of International Exchange Regulations, which governs the inflow of financial capital and guarantees investors access to the formal exchange market, when the investment is less than $5 million.

[2] At present, around 90 percent of investors are subject to the national tax regimen, with a 15 percent tax on profits.

DL 600 was promulgated in 1974 and has since been modified six times: in 1981, 1985, 1987, 1989, 1990, and most recently in March, 1993 (Table 3.1). Although six changes in 20 years may appear to be an excessive number, it should be noted that these changes have not been very significant. For instance, the most recent modification reduced from three years to one year the capital repatriation period, clarified certain concepts regarding access to the formal foreign exchange market and investors' tax charge, reduced the tax rate on profits (from 49.5 percent down to 42 percent) of investors opting for the tax invariability regimen, and effected certain changes in the composition of the Foreign Investment Committee.

Therefore, it can be truly said that regulations on FDI in Chile have remained extremely stable since their 1974 reform. Furthermore, from the description of DL 600, one may rightly conclude that these regulations have been decidedly favorable to FDI. This stability and favorability in the Chilean institutional framework has in fact created the necessary conditions for the sizable increases in FDI that have taken place since 1986.

Chapter XIX was implemented with a dual purpose in mind—namely, to lower Chile's external debt (which in the mid-1980s constituted a serious economic policy problem) and to increase FDI inflows into the country. The Chapter XIX mechanism allowed foreign investors to purchase Chilean external debt titles (of significantly lower world market value lower than the face value), which were then used as capital for investing in Chile. Chile's Central Bank valuated the titles at 100 percent of their original value (minus a discount) and exchanged them for titles in Chilean pesos (at the official exchange rate), tradable on Chile's capital market, thus enabling the investor to use the funds in an authorized investment. It should be mentioned that by law, only 10 percent of investments in the mining sector could be financed this way. In addition, unlike DL 600, Chapter XIX investment projects were subject to strict evaluation criteria by the authorities. Priority tended to be given to investments in sectors that would help to expand Chile's export supply or contribute to specific public policy objectives. In other words, Chapter XIX exercised much greater discretionality than DL 600. In addition, the Chapter XIX program's directing body, in terms of approving projects and their amounts, was the Central Bank and not the Foreign Investment Committee (ECLAC, 1990).

Chapter XIX was at its most relevant during the late 1980s, when external debt titles were still being sold on the world market at significant discounts. Once the certificates' market value began to approach their face value—which occurred in 1991—investors stopped using Chapter XIX. Chapter XIX investments were more costly to investors than were DL 600 investments in terms of capital repatriation (the minimum duration of Chapter XIX investments was 10 years) and profit remittances (which could not be carried out until five years had lapsed). Both of these time terms have recently been liberalized (in 1992 and

Table 3.1. Major Modifications to DL 600

Date	Modification
December 10, 1981	Appoints the Executive Secretariat of the Central Bank's Foreign Investment Committee
November 30, 1985	Introduces taxation-related improvements
December 31, 1987	Introduces Art. 7 bis, which provides for the option of an invariable 40 percent tax rate plus a variable supplement
October 10, 1989	Central Bank's Institutional Constitutive law
January 25, 1990	Establishes the structure of the Foreign Investment Committee (CIE)
March 31, 1993	Lowers to one year the time terms on capital remittance. Provides that there will no time terms on repatriation of capital increases stemming from profits. Provides that the Executive Vice-President's approval is needed for access to the formal capital market for purposes of remitting profits or repatriating capital. Changes Art. 6 to read "investment carried out" and not "investment authorized." Repeals Art. 7 bis and sets the maximum invariable tax rate at 42 percent.

Source: Authors' compilation, based on official documents.

Table 3.2. Foreign Investment, 1985–93

(US$ millions per year)

	DL 600[a]	Chapter XIX[b]	Total
1985	114	30	144
1986	194	199	383
1987	414	701	1,115
1988	526	886	1,412
1989	495	1,321	1,816
1990	998	412	1,410
1991	899	-37	862
1992	788	-32	756
1993[c]	1,617	-50	1,567

Sources: Central Bank of Chile and Foreign-Investment Committee.
[a] Investment realized. It includes associated credits and amortization and profit reinvestment, as well as investments made under Chapter XIV of the Central Bank's Compendium of International Exchange Regulations.
[b] Includes investment via Appendix 2 of Chapter XIX, on funds of investment societies.
[c] Provisional figures.

1993), in order to relieve the pressure toward currency appreciation caused by the voluminous inflows of capital (Agosin, Fuentes and Letelier, 1994).

Evolution of FDI, 1987–93

Table 3.2 shows the evolution of FDI from 1985 to 1993 in its two main modalities. Chapter XIX, it will be remembered, did not really begin to have a significant impact until 1986, with an investment of $199 million recorded that year. Nevertheless, during the 1987–93 period, Chapter XIX investments came to represent 36 percent of total cumulative FDI inflows. With respect to total foreign investment, the 1987–93 period accounted for 74 percent of the cumulative FDI inflows of the entire 1974–93 period—$9.919 billion. The largest inflows occurred in 1989 and then declined sharply because of the sudden decrease in investments made through the Chapter XIX mechanism (as a result of the rise in the market value of Chilean external debt titles), reaching a low point in 1992. In 1993, FDI finally began to pick up once again.

If we look only at the foreign investments carried out through DL 600, such investments reached a temporary high in 1990, then declined through 1992, once again to surge to a new high in 1993. Partial data available for 1994 indicate that the year's FDI inflows were on the order of $3 billion—a record level. Even when Chapter XIX was functioning at its peak (1986–90), FDI inflows through DL 600 continued growing significantly (from $184 million in 1986 to $1.184 billion in 1990), which suggests that there was no significant degree of substitution between inflows through Chapter XIX and inflows through DL 600. In other

Figure 3.1. Chile: Foreign Direct Investment by Modality, 1987-93

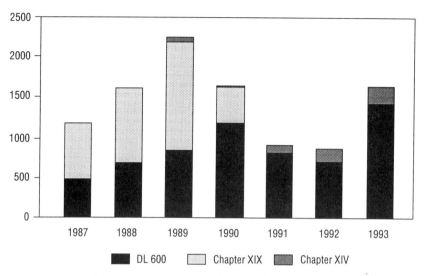

Source: Authors' compilation using data from the Foreign Investment Committee and the Central Bank of Chile.

words, most of the funds that entered through Chapter XIX would not have entered through DL 600.

Figure 3.1 shows the evolution of investments that entered Chile through these two mechanisms (plus those realized under Chapter XIV of the Compendium of International Exchange Regulations of the Central Bank). In the figure we can see that FDI declined in 1990, largely because of the diminished attractiveness of Chapter XIX—an overall downward trend that continued until 1992. We also see that FDI through DL 600 also declined in 1991, then took an upward direction once again in 1993.

The importance of FDI to the Chilean economy and to gross capital formation reached its zenith in the late 1980s, when FDI amounted to nearly 6 percent of GDP and one-fourth of gross capital formation (Table 3.3). In large measure, this was the result of the special one-time-only situation created by the capitalization of the external debt. In more recent years and as a result of the dwindling of possibilities offered by the debt conversion program, such motivation has diminished significantly. Nevertheless, FDI currently has a much greater relative weight in the economy than it did before the zenith of 1987–93. In 1985, FDI inflows were less than 1 percent of GDP and only 5 percent of gross capital formation, in comparison with 3.6 percent and 13.8 percent, respectively, in 1993.

Table 3.3. Foreign Investment as a Percentage of GDP and of Gross Investment, 1985–93

Year	FDI/GDP	FDI/total investment
1985	0.9	5.1
1986	1.9	11.4
1987	4.7	24.2
1988	5.2	25.7
1989	5.8	25.3
1990	4.6	18.9
1991	2.5	11.4
1992	1.8	7.6
1993	3.6	13.8

Sources: Central Bank and Foreign-Investment Committee.

Sectoral Evolution

Analysis of the sectoral distribution of FDI will give some insight into its objectives. First we shall disaggregate FDI in accordance with the nine main sectors of the Standard International Classification (SITC), and then focus in more detail on the industrial sector. The following sectors will be considered: agriculture, forestry and fishing; mining; manufacturing; energy; construction; trade; transport and communications; financial services; and social and personal services.

To begin, let us analyze the sectoral distribution of Chapter XIX FDI from 1987 to 1991 (since 1991, no FDI has entered Chile through this mechanism). The pertinent figures are presented in Table 3.4.

Total inflows during the 1987–91 period (Figure 3.2 and the last column of Table 3.4) show that the industrial sector attracted the largest share of resources (31 percent), followed by the agricultural sector (29.5 percent). If we consider the agricultural, mining and industrial sectors as being essentially tradables sectors, then the overwhelming majority of foreign resources went into tradables (74 percent). The financial services sector also received a significant percentage of Chapter XIX FDI. Because the period under examination is quite short (only five years), it would not be reasonable to undertake a very detailed analysis of the time trend of these percentages. Nevertheless, Figure 3.3 shows that the tradables sectors (defined basically as agriculture, mining, and industry) received significantly more Chapter XIX FDI than did the nontradable goods sectors through the period, with the participation by the nontradables sectors showing a steady increase.

Table 3.5 presents the sectoral distribution of the 1987–93 period's FDI inflows through the DL 600 mechanism. Chile's mining sector attracted the great-

113

Table 3.4. Sectoral Share of Chapter XIX FDI, 1987–91
(Percentages)

Sector	1987	1988	1989	1990	1991	Total
Agriculture	64.2	24.3	19.4	15.4	—	29.5
Mining	6.8	12.7	13.5	23.9	—	13.1
Industry	6.3	40.7	39.7	23.4	46.2	31.0
Energy	9.9	1.6	0.0	0.0	—	2.5
Trade	5.4	1.2	5.7	4.5	—	4.3
Transport	0.4	4.6	9.4	9.2	—	6.2
Financial services	5.8	12.3	10.4	23.4	53.9	11.7
Other services	1.2	2.7	1.8	0.2	—	1.7
Total	100.0	100.0	100.0	100.0	100.0	100.0
Total (in US$ millions)	690.2	890.1	1,313.6	404.8	10.8	3,308.5

Source: Central Bank of Chile.

Figure 3.2. Chile: Sectoral Distribution of Chapter XIX FDI, 1987-91
(Percentages)

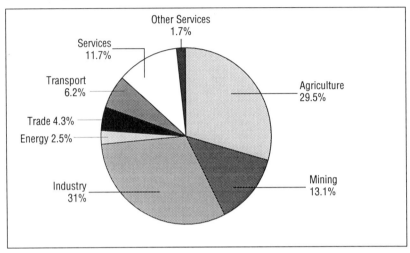

Source: Authors' compilation using data from the Central Bank of Chile.

Figure 3.3. Chile: Chapter XIX FDI, Tradables and Nontradables, 1987-91
(Percentages)

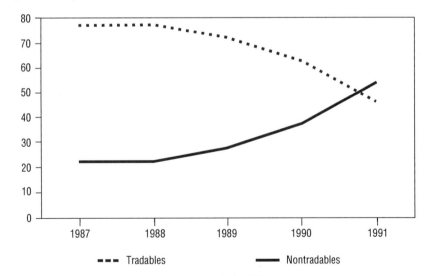

Source: Authors' compilation using data from the Central Bank of Chile.

Table 3.5. DL 600ª FDI's Sectoral Distribution, 1987–93
(Percentages)

Sector	1987	1988	1989	1990	1991	1992	1993b	Total
Agriculture	1.2	0.4	0.6	3.2	3.3	2.2	2.6	2.0
Mining	49.7	55.0	79.4	75.4	48.9	59.7	46.1	59.3
Industry	19.1	4.5	7.9	9.1	22.5	11.3	31.0	15.8
Construction	1.6	0.3	0.9	0.5	3.6	2.5	1.4	1.5
Trade	10.1	0.3	1.2	0.8	4.7	3.7	3.9	3.1
Transport	0.3	33.0	0.5	0.7	3.6	5.0	4.0	6.5
Financial services	17.9	6.5	9.6	10.2	12.6	16.3	10.6	11.4
Other services	0.06	0.08	0.02	0.06	0.89	0.39	0.45	0.30
Total	100.0	100.0	100.0	100.0	100.0	100.0	100.0	100.0
Total (in US$ millions)	541.3	845.2	969.7	1,321.8	953.9	995.7	1,306.8	6,934.4

Source: Foreign-Investment Committee. The energy sector presented no "effected investment."
ª The definition of sectors does not fully coincide with that of the Foreign-Investment Committee.
b Through October 1993. Because of minor revisions, there are some discrepancies compared to Table 3.2 figures.

est percentage of these DL 600 inflows, receiving nearly 60 percent of the total. It is important to note that the mining sector's participation was strongly enhanced by the *La Escondida* copper mine project, which boosted the sector's shares of DL 600 FDI to 79 percent and 75 percent of the respective totals for 1989 and 1990 (years in which an important portion of total DL 600 FDI occurred). The mining sector's participation in 1989 and 1990 was, in fact, almost double that of 1988 and 1991, the years immediately preceding and following.

The financial sector's share has been rising in both nominal dollar and percentage terms. This sector's increased receipt of DL 600 FDI is in part a response to the gradual development of the capital market; in turn, these same FDI inflows contributed a great deal to the deepening of the financial sector. Finally, the manufacturing industry experienced fluctuations in its share of FDI in part because of the volatility of the inflows into mining and in part because of the large fluctuations in the amounts entering the industrial sector. More than $100 million in FDI went into the country's manufacturing industry in 1987—a figure that declined to $38 million in 1988, rallied to $70 million in 1989, and then dramatically shot up to over $400 million in 1993, or 31 percent of the year's FDI total.

Figure 3.4 and Figure 3.5 show the sectoral share and the tradables versus nontradables distribution, respectively. The tradables sectors attained their peak DL 600 FDI share in 1989, then experienced a slow decline until 1992, and once again showed an upturn in 1993.

In comparing both FDI modalities—Chapter XIX and DL 600—it is immediately apparent that the mining sector's share of DL 600 FDI was much greater than its share of Chapter XIX FDI. The explanation is quite simple and resides in the fact that Chapter XIX established restrictions on participating investors' investments in the mining sector. Another interesting contrast—and one without any simple explanation—relates to the agricultural sector, which received only a marginal portion (2 percent) of the FDI inflows that entered through Decree Law 600 but about 30 percent of the FDI inflows that entered through Chapter XIX. In turn, the manufacturing industry captured a larger share of Chapter XIX FDI than it did of DL 600 FDI, in part because of the effect of the mining sector and in part because the debt conversion program made a deliberate effort to direct investment toward the industrial sector, and preferably toward export activities. It is interesting to note that 31 percent of the period's total Chapter XIX FDI inflows were effectively channeled into industry, as compared to only 16 percent of total DL 600 FDI inflows.

Figure 3.6 shows that when we combine Chapter XIX FDI inflows with DL 600 FDI inflows, the overall result is that the mining sector and the industrial sector were the recipients of the largest amount of foreign resources during the 1987–93 period. The tradables producing sectors, for their part, received 75 percent of the same period's total FDI inflows.

Figure 3.4. Chile: DL 600 FDI by Sector, 1987-93
(Percentages)

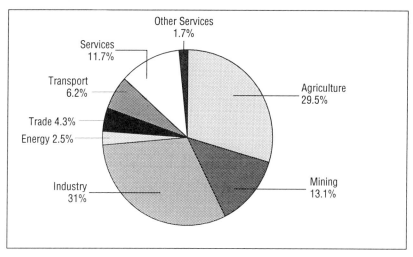

Source: Authors' compilation using data from the Foreign Investment Committee.

Figure 3.5. Chile: DL 600 FDI, Tradables and Nontradables, 1987-91
(Percentages)

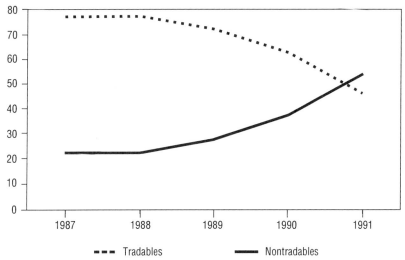

Source: Authors' compilation using data from the Foreign Investment Committee.

Figure 3.6. Chile: Total FDI, 1987-93
(Percentages)

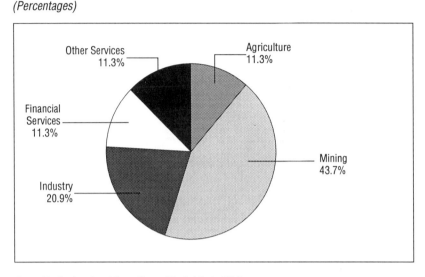

Source: Foreign Investment Committee and Central Bank of Chile.

Manufacturing Sector

Let us now turn to an examination of the distribution of foreign investment within the manufacturing sector and its corresponding subsectors during the 1987–93 period. Table 3.6, which shows disaggregated distribution of DL 600 FDI, indicates that the chemicals and pharmaceutical subsector (35) attracted the largest foreign investment flows within the manufacturing sector during the period. It should be noted that the large share of this subsector stems from numerous projects (30 companies received FDI) and a few megaprojects (in this period only one project absorbed more than $100 million, and two others involved investments greater than $40 million). Meanwhile, subsector 34, corresponding to paper and derivatives, received only an insignificant share until 1988, when it suddenly became, for several years (1989, 1990 and 1992), the major FDI recipient; in this case, unlike sector 35, the increase resulted from investments in three megaprojects. The food and beverages industries (31) and, to a lesser extent, the textiles, leather and footwear industries (32) and the wood and furniture industries (33) also received significant inflows of investment. Thus it would seem that, within the manufacturing sector, the subsectors that tended to receive the largest shares of FDI were those in which Chile has comparative advantages based upon natural resources and low wages.

Table 3.6. Disaggregated Distribution of DL 600 FDI within the Manufacturing Sector, 1987–93
(Percentages)

Code	1987	1988	1989	1990	1991	1992	1993	Total
31	8.2	15.8	21.5	29.4	6.2	19.3	19.3	16.5
32	0.1	1.9	0.8	4.6	3.5	0.9	26.8	11.8
33	0.4	41.2	11.2	7.6	31.5	14.3	2.5	11.8
34	0.2	0.9	36.6	34.2	24.3	25.3	16.1	19.6
35	14.7	12.3	10.3	16.2	31.8	12.7	31.4	24.2
36	3.0	1.0	9.5	0.2	0.2	0.0	0.8	1.4
37	0.4	0.1	0.0	0.0	1.1	9.3	1.4	1.8
38	18.7	26.7	9.2	6.8	0.9	8.5	1.6	5.9
39	54.3	0.1	0.8	0.9	0.5	9.7	0.3	6.9
Total	100.0	100.0	100.0	100.0	100.0	100.0	100.0	100.0
Total (in US$ millions)	103.5	38.0	69.6	96.6	202.5	105.3	398.6	1,014.1

Source: Foreign-Investment Committee.

Table 3.7 presents the same information, but with reference to the investments channeled through the mechanism of Chapter XIX. In this case, one subsector (34, paper and derivatives) absorbed 61 percent of all investment as a result of three megaprojects (Rozas, 1992). The food and beverages subsector (31) also captured an important share of this investment. Although we note that FDI resources via Chapter XIX went largely into the same industrial subsectors as did FDI resources via DL 600, in the case of Chapter XIX the concentration is more intense. Comparing the figures from Table 3.6 and Table 3.7 shows that of all the investment destined for the manufacturing sector, 84 percent focused on subsectors 31 through 35 in the case of DL 600 and 98 percent in the case of Chapter XIX. By the same token, the industrial subsectors receiving the smallest shares of DL 600 FDI were the same ones that received the smallest shares of Chapter XIX FDI—namely, the most technologically sophisticated subsectors (37, 38 and 39, which include basic metal manufacturers and producers of metal products, equipment and machinery). In other words, the application of the debt conversion program to foreign investments in manufacturing results in a more intense subsectoral concentration than does the entry of such FDI through DL 600, but the receiving sectors tended to be the same.

Put still another way, although we can observe greater sectoral concentration in the investments made through Chapter XIX versus those made through DL 600 (in part, through deliberate policy decisions), the subsectors toward which foreign investors were primarily oriented in both cases were those closely linked to the country's natural resource base and to its traditional comparative advantages.

Table 3.7. Chapter XIX FDI within the Manufacturing Sector, 1987–91
(Percentages)

Code	1987	1988	1989	1990	1991	Total
31	32.1	16.0	20.9	17.5	—	19.2
32	29.9	4.9	2.4	—	—	4.2
33	6.1	7.9	2.8	10.2	—	5.4
34	5.9	61.0	65.6	59.6	100.0	61.0
35	20.9	6.2	7.9	12.8	—	8.2
36	—	—	—	—	—	—
37	—	2.4	—	—	—	0.8
38	—	1.3	0.5	—	—	0.7
39	5.0	0.3	—	—	—	0.3
Total	100.0	100.0	100.0	100.0	100.0	1
Total (in US$ millions)	43.8	361.8	520.4	94.6	5.0	1,025.6

Source: Central Bank.

Causes of the Recent Increase in FDI

Two research methods were used to explain the increase in foreign direct investment during the 1987–93 period. The first was an econometric analysis of FDI inflows in real terms for the 1975–92 period, and the second used the results of a survey of companies with recent foreign investments.

Empirical Model for the Analysis of FDI

Our econometric analysis set out to find the variables that, from a statistical point of view, best explain the behavior of FDI in the period following implementation of promarket reforms in Chile. In accordance with an analysis by Ros (1994), the most relevant variables are national economic conditions, country risk as perceived by investors, and economic policies.[3] As an indicator of Chile's national economic conditions, the model employed the level of real GDP. The expected sign of the coefficient associated with this variable is positive. Country risk was

---

[3] In an analysis of FDI in Mexico, Ros (1994) also includes variables that takes into account the attractiveness of investing in the United States, the principal country of origin of FDI in Mexico. Thus it was that the U.S. manufacturing industry's degree of installed-capacity utilization (measured as the ratio between the observed manufacturing sector product and its potential product) came to be used as a variable to help explain FDI in Mexico. But in the case of Chile, it is not necessary to factor in a variable of this type, because the origin of FDI in Chile is quite varied and Chile is a small recipient country. By the way, these facts made it very unlikely that the worldwide recession in recent years has significantly affected the FDI levels in Chile.

represented by Chile's debt-to-exports ratio; the higher this ratio, the higher the probability that a balance-of-payments crisis will oblige the authorities to impose restrictions on profit remittances and capital repatriation. Another variable that was included was the real exchange rate. Considering that FDI has gone predominantly into the sectors that produce tradable goods, an anticipated rise in the real exchange rate, by making those sectors more profitable, would draw FDI flows toward them.[4] Since there was no estimate of the expected exchange rate, the observed real exchange rate was used. And finally, a dummy variable was used to capture the effect of Chapter XIX. This variable has a value of 1 in the years 1986–90—the period in which investors made use of the Chapter XIX mechanism—and a value of 0 in other years. This variable was included in the estimates interactively with real GDP.

The model ended up estimating the following equation:

$$FDI^* = a_0 + a_1 Y^* + a_2 D_1 Y^* + a_3 CR + a_4 RER \qquad (1)$$

where

FDI^* = FDI in current dollars, deflated by the U.S. wholesale price index;

Y^* = GDP in current prices, converted to current dollars and deflated by the U.S. wholesale price index;

D_1 = dummy variable with a value of 1 in the 1986–90 period and a value of 0 in other years;

CR = country risk, for which the model used the ratio between external debt and exports of goods and services; and

RER = nominal exchange rate, deflated by the Chilean consumer price index and multiplied by the U.S. wholesale price index

The results of the ordinary-least-squares estimate were as follows:

$$FDI^* = 376.6 + 0.02Y^* + 0.04D_1 Y^* - 1.46CR + 8.28RER \qquad (1a)$$
$$(-0.90) \quad (2.12) \quad (4.79) \quad (-1.99) \quad (1.90)$$

adjusted $R^2 = 0.890$; Durbin Watson = 2.07;
t statistics in parentheses

As can be seen, the coefficients associated with these variables have the expected signs and differ from zero to acceptable levels of significance, and the

---

[4] It is unlikely that the real exchange rate would affect certain investments that have been very important in Chile (such as mining sector investments), since their profitability is high in a broad real exchange rate range. But marginally, the real exchange rate is a determining factor in the profitability of exportable goods.

equation accounts for nearly 90 percent of the variation in FDI.[5] In accordance with the estimates of the parameters of equation (1a), the Chapter XIX mechanism had an important catalytic effect on foreign investment in Chile: the effect of the national economy's size (the coefficient associated with the variable Y^*) upon real levels of FDI doubled during the period in which investors used Chapter XIX.

Qualitative Analysis

A second approach to examining the causes of FDI's behavior in Chile between 1987 and 1993 is based upon a qualitative analysis. To this end, researchers carried out a survey of 15 foreign investors (or their representatives) that operate in Chile in the most diverse economic sectors.[6] The objective of the survey was to discover these firms' motivation for investing in Chile, as well as to measure the impact that such investment had upon the country's development.

With respect to the factors that affected the decision to invest in Chile, the impression given by the survey responses seems to be that the companies pursue business in different parts of the world for reasons of overall business strategy and that the chosen recipient countries need to have demonstrated a combination of profitability and investment security. In other words, the important thing for foreign investors was the possibility of creating projects that would be profitable and that would represent an acceptable level of risk. In that sense, the existence of reasonable and stable FDI laws and other related economic policies and the adoption of an external debt conversion mechanism very favorable to foreign investors have been factors fostering investment flows, which have been much more voluminous than in the past. Nevertheless, these have been only contributing factors. Other key factors in the Chilean case have been the abundance of high-quality natural resources and a rapidly expanding domestic market (an important factor for investors in certain sectors such as financial services).

The existence of profitable investment projects in Chile is also directly related to various additional economic policies applied since the mid-1970s. For instance, the development of the country's own capital market—associated in part with the privatization of social security through the creation of the Pension Fund Administrators (AFP)—generated profitable new projects not only in these new companies but throughout the country's entire financial sector. In fact, ever since the second half of the 1970s, there has been a gradual liberalization of

[5] The only observable econometric problem is a certain degree of multicolinearity, since the *CR* and *RER* variables are related: during the debt crisis (1983–87), the real exchange rate depreciated sharply. Nevertheless, the degree of colinearity is not high.

[6] The original intention was to survey 25 investors, but several companies did not participate, for various reasons. Time limits did not permit researchers to interview other enterprises in their stead.

foreign capital access to Chile's national financial sector. At present, foreign capital is subject only to reasonable precautionary criteria—the same ones that apply to domestic capital—before being allowed access. It comes as no surprise, then, that the financial sector has been one of the major recipients of FDI, led only by mining and by other more recently developed export sectors (especially the forestry and the cellulose and paper sectors).

Considering that the laws on FDI in Chile became very liberal and stable as far back as 1974, why was it only in the second half of the 1980s that FDI finally began to increase very rapidly? This question has two answers, neither one sufficient in itself. First, it took time for the new laws on FDI to bear fruit. As mentioned earlier, DL 600 has been in effect since 1974, and there has clearly been a learning period for recipients and investors alike. Not only that, but FDI's performance during those early years was strongly affected by the period's economic events. Moreover, toward the end of this ten-year learning period, in 1982, GDP began to decline sharply in response to the debt crisis, and there was an associated decrease in all inflows of foreign capital including FDI. Foreign investment did not recover from this shock until the Chilean economy and the balance of payments had shown clear signs of overcoming the crisis. Only in 1986 did the country's economy begin to bounce back, aided by a surge in world copper prices starting in 1987 and by the 1986 world oil price decline. All of these latter factors finally led to the appearance of profitable businesses in the economy—businesses that attracted foreign investors. The second part of our answer (as to the cause of the lag) can be found in the fact that it was not until late in 1985 that the Chilean government began to apply the conversion program. The large implicit subsidy to foreign investors was destined to have a large positive impact upon investment inflows, particularly in the context of the recuperation of the economy and the recovering balance of payments.

The country risk factor undoubtedly has been a pivotal concept in all of this. In addition to the resurgence of the economy and the brightening of the external payments picture (which helped to decrease the country risk in investors' eyes), the perception of the durability of adjustment-related reforms was probably enhanced by the fact that as of the late 1980s the reform process no longer seemed as vulnerable to external shocks, and also by the expected return to democratic governmental institutions.

Another key factor has been, of course, the role played by Chile's aforementioned external debt conversion program. Investment would probably have arrived even without the program, but it would have arrived later. One might credibly argue that the sectoral distribution of FDI suggests that such investment really needed no special incentives, since it flowed primarily into sectors in which Chile enjoys obvious comparative advantages—sectors that, accordingly, would have been profitable to foreign investors even without special subsidies. Nevertheless, the program clearly attracted the interest of foreign investors at a crucial moment when the economy had not yet overcome the external crisis. Further-more, since these new foreign investments via Chapter XIX were oriented largely toward nonmining export sectors, the program helped to relieve Chile's external sector blockage, reducing foreign debt levels and increasing exports. The pro-gram can be deemed successful, furthermore, judging by the fact that FDI levels have continued to rise, even without the subsidy.

In summary, then, factors that played an important role in the recent upsurge in foreign direct investment include the stability of the rules of play within a general legal framework favorable to foreign investment, overcoming the debt crisis, and the opportune adoption of an external debt conversion program that turned out to be temporary.

FDI's Contribution to Development

This section analyzes the impact that FDI has had on the development process of Chile—particularly on capital formation, since it has been one of the factors that have historically limited the growth of the Chilean economy. In addition, be-cause of the external sector's great importance to an economy with a small do-mestic market, special attention will also be given to examining FDI's role in the expansion and diversification of Chilean exports. Finally, the section looks at the contribution of foreign enterprises to the economy in terms of introducing new products and technologies to the Chilean production sector and the formation of human capital.

Contribution to the Formation of Physical Capital

Quantitative Analysis

Investment is one of the basic elements of the economic adjustment programs to which high priority has been given by most Latin American countries. These economic adjustment programs seek to increase an economy's growth possibili-ties by a permanent change in relative prices. This change in relative prices would favor the accumulation of capital and, thus, greater growth. The need to achieve greater macroeconomic stability is linked to the requirement of making growth sustainable by means of a permanent increase in investment and savings. In or-der to implement long-term adjustment measures, it is of fundamental impor-tance to have a framework of principles that will permit an understanding of the investment process and its determinants, particularly those that can be regulated to some degree by specific policies. In view of the new realities created by an open economy engaged in an intensifying process of internationalization, it be-comes even more important to study the effects of FDI upon national investment.

The use of an empirical model to explain the behavior of total investment *(TI)* should take into account several factors. On the one hand there are factors linked to the behavior of the domestic economy, and on the other, the effects associated with foreign direct investment. With respect to the factors related to the behavior of the domestic economy, TI will basically respond to price factors and aggregate product factors. In this sense, internal investment *(II)* responds to changes in Tobin's Q (empirically approximated by the general index of real prices of traded shares) and to changes in lagged values of GDP (a variable that basically reflects the "accelerator" effect). Therefore,

$$II_t = II(Q_{t-1}, Y_{t-1}), \tag{2}$$

where t represents the period being examined, t-1 the corresponding lag, and Y the level of real GDP.

In this context, *II* is the investment made by Chilean residents, such that if we add to it the investments made by foreigners in physical assets, it seems we should be able to obtain total investment *(TI)*. FDI does not, however, correspond simply to foreigners' investments in physical assets. It also includes the purchase of existing assets, payment for trademarks, related credits, and the like. Even so, part of FDI does correspond to the addition of physical assets, and therefore it is possible to express a function of total investment *TI* (by domestic and foreign agents), estimated empirically as

$$TI_t = TI(Q_{t-1}, Y_{t-1}, FDI_{t-1}), \tag{3}$$

The econometric analysis was performed using Almon's polynomial-lags method. The results of the estimation of this relationship by the ordinary least-squares method (OLS),[7] as presented in Table 3.8, indicate that around 98 percent of the total variation in investment can be explained on the basis of this model. The three variables are significant to 1 percent, and the elasticities that are obtained are statistically significant: with respect to Q, investment's percentual response would be 0.24, while for GDP it would reach 0.49. The elasticity of total investment to FDI is only 0.06. The equation in question appears to reproduce more or less adequately the observed behavior (Figure 3.7).[8]

---

[7] Since the equation's right-side variables are exogenous in each period t (because Q and Y are lagged) and since FDI is assumed to be exogenous, the equation can be estimated by ordinary least squares.

[8] Although the estimation in Table 3.8 shows a Durbin-Watson test result in the "inconclusive" zone and although in correcting with the AR(1) method the results show much instability, we still use these results as the basis for the analysis because there exists no evidence either for or against the autocorrelation hypothesis.

Table 3.8. Explanation of the Variation in Log TI
(ordinary least squares, Almon's polynomial-lag technique)

	C	LQ	LGDP	LFDI
t	3.95			0.038
	(12.30)			(2.795)
t-1		0.008	0.011	0.021
		(0.229)	(0.142)	(4.374)
t-2		0.050	0.086	0.003
		(3.730)	(3.001)	(0.249)
t-3		0.070	0.129	
		(3.240)	(2.936)	
t-4		0.069	0.142	
		(3.342)	(3.592)	
t-5		0.046	1.122	
		(1.729)	(2.253)	
Sum of coefficients		0.245	0.492	0.063
		(16.755)	(15.204)	(4.374)

Source: Author calculations.
Note: Adjusted R^2 = 0.98; Durbin Watson = 1.112; N = 36; t statistic in parentheses.

The evidence presented in the analysis of the determinants of FDI suggests a degree of endogeneity between *TI* (through its impact on real GDP) and FDI that should be taken into account in the empirical estimations. Thus, the regression in which total investment was estimated (as a function of Tobin's Q, GDP and FDI) should be estimated using methods that are appropriate to the fact of the endogeneity of FDI. The results, shown in Table 3.9, show the details of such an estimation.[9] The instruments used were the variations in GDP movable average and in inflation (important signals for FDI), a dummy variable for the Chapter XIX period, and the lagged values of the exogenous variables. As can be observed, the results fall in general within the range of the results obtained through the OLS method (Table 3.8), corroborating the fit presented in Figure 3.7.

In summary, then, the role that FDI plays in total investment is important, although the effects of profitability and growth (measured by Tobin's Q and the accelerator effect) are quantitatively more important. Considering the problem as a system, there also exists a multiplier that reflects the effect of macroeconomic adjustment on total investment (measured, for instance, by the real exchange

[9] The estimation in question was performed using a two-stage least-squares approach.

Figure 3.7. Chile: Investment Model: Adjusted vs. Actual, 1983-91

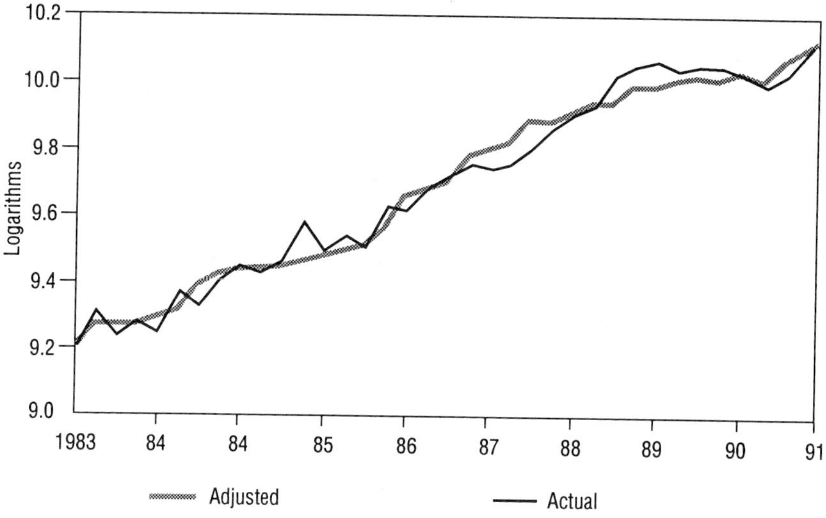

Adjusted   Actual

Source: Authors' estimates.

rate's effect on FDI and by FDI's own effect on total investment), which serves to underscore macroeconomic policy's significant effect on total investment. The results permit us to emphasize the significance of the role that stability should play as a prerequisite for the achievement of expanded investment and accelerated growth.

Qualitative Analysis

From the interviews conducted for the present study, it can be concluded that foreign investors have had a positive impact upon the formation of physical capital (machinery and structures). In the majority of cases (67 percent of the firms surveyed), the initial investment or the payment for existing assets constituted only a fraction of the investment carried out later. In several cases the initial investment was made as a means of getting to know the market, and the more significant investment did not occur until later. This phenomenon holds true for new investments as well as for the purchase of existing assets. From this standpoint, there seems to be little basis for the negative judgment with respect to FDI destined toward the purchase of existing assets. The key is to observe capital formation within a relatively long time span. If today there occurs, for instance, a foreign investment consisting only of the purchase of existing assets, then capital

Table 3.9. Instrumental-variable-based Explanation of the Variation in Log TI
(instruments used: (C, VARGDP, VARINF, PDL 9, PDL 10, PDL 11, PDL 12, PDL 13, PDL 14, PDL 15, PDL 16)

	C	LQ	LGDP	LFDI
t	4.328			0.006
	(7.897)			(0.102)
t-1		0.019	0.031	0.023
		(0.398)	(0.312)	(3.772)
t-2		0.048	0.073	0.040
		(3.083)	(2.193)	(0.718)
t-3		0.062	0.103	
		(2.347)	(1.703)	
t-4		0.061	0.121	
		(2.294)	(2.129)	
t-5		0.044	10.126	
		(1.402)	(2.025)	
Sum of coefficients		0.236	0.457	0.069
		(13.01)	(8.982)	(3.772)

Source: Author calculations.
Note: Adjusted R^2 = 0.96; Durbin Watson = 1.27; N = 36; t statistic in parentheses.
PDL 9, 10, and 11 correspond to lags of LQ, used as instruments.
PDL 12, 13, and 14 correspond to lags of LGDP, used as instruments.
PDL 15, 16, and 17 correspond to lags of DR, used as instruments.

formation could conceivably constitute for now only a small fraction of the associated FDI inflow (the size of this fraction would depend on the use that the seller of the existing assets makes of the purchase money received). If during the next year, however, the plant is expanded, then an addition will have been made to Chile's physical capital. The relevant comparison becomes that between this investment and any additional investment that would have been made by the local owner. In this regard, it should be pointed out that foreign investors generally have better access to external credit than do national firms (especially medium-sized national firms) and that the cost of capital is usually much lower for a foreign firm than for a national firm. These facts imply that investment levels of foreign enterprises that decide to invest in one of the countries of the region can be higher than the levels of investment that would have been made by similar enterprises of national origin.

For the foregoing reasons, our impression is that the distinction often made between new foreign investment and foreigners' purchase of existing assets is not entirely relevant. In this sense, it does not seem reasonable to limit the purchase of existing assets. If a foreigner wishes to purchase an already-functioning enterprise, then that purchaser is presumably paying an amount at least as large as the current net value of the future profits of the former owners. If the foreign purchaser is willing to pay that amount, it is probably because of being able to generate even greater profits or because of having a lower discount rate—or both. In both cases, a positive impact is produced upon Chile's economic development in general and upon the country's capital formation in particular. In order to obtain these larger profits, the foreign purchaser of the already-functioning Chilean enterprise will have to make further investments, and a similar phenomenon also occurs in regard to the purchaser's access to a lower discount rate (lower costs of capital imply greater investment).

FDI's Contribution to Chile's Access to International Markets

Earlier we described FDI's recent evolution, including distribution of the investment between the sectors producing tradable goods and those producing nontradable goods. In general terms, most of the FDI has gone into the tradables sectors. The evolution of this tendency has been steady over time, as can be observed in Figure 3.3 and Figure 3.5, showing FDI that entered through Chapter XIX and through DL 600, respectively. Figure 3.6, which presents total FDI's 1987–93 distribution between tradables and nontradables, shows that the tradable goods sectors (mining, the manufacturing industry and agriculture) received 75 percent of all FDI. All of this goes to show that FDI has gone primarily into Chile's tradable goods sectors, primarily exportable goods.

Our survey of FDI firms served to bolster this finding. Some 73 percent of the interviewed firms produce tradable goods, oriented principally toward the external market. Of the interviewed companies classified as tradable goods producers, some 36 percent have introduced a new product into Chile's array of export offerings. In addition, 36 percent of the interviewed companies that were exporters had increased the number of countries to which they exported following the investment.

It should be noted that even the interviewed FDI enterprises in the services sector have had an impact on exports. Foreign banks are quite likely to have a greater knowledge of external markets than do national banks, and foreign companies in Chile's tourism subsector are probably better positioned than are national companies for attracting visitors to Chile. In the case of banking, the interviewed executives believed that their banks have a better knowledge of certain markets than do Chile's domestic banks or that they have branches in markets in which the domestic banking firms are not present. These same executives stated that in both arenas their banks have opened new markets for Chilean exports and that they have therefore had an indirect impact on the country's export diversification process. In the case of tourism, where FDI is growing in importance, the impact of FDI has not been so much upon the creation of new export markets as upon the creation of new "exportable" products. Tourism brings in foreign exchange by attracting foreign tourists, and foreign tourists are more likely to visit the country if they can have access to hotels belonging to international chains, because of the quality assurance that such hotels provide. Therefore, in this case, too, FDI has generated a positive impact upon the country's array of "exportable" products.

As noted earlier, foreign investment has focused primarily upon export sectors in which Chile has traditional comparative advantages (mining) or upon sectors closely tied to the country's natural resource base (forestry products or cellulose and paper). In the case of the latter sectors, FDI has contributed to export diversification and to reduction of copper's comparative share in total exports vis-à-vis copper's mid-1970s export share. Nevertheless, in only exceptional cases have investments by exporting companies added to Chile's array of exportable goods any products technologically more sophisticated than the products exported by those same companies before the foreign investment. Therefore, although the recent FDI's impact upon Chile's position in the world market has been positive overall, it has not been as beneficial as had been hoped for in this particular regard (see, for instance, Ozawa, 1992, and Agosin and Prieto, 1993). In contrast, nearly all of the foreign investment in places such as Korea, Singapore, Taiwan or Thailand is oriented toward exports of manufactured products (GATT, 1991; Ariff and Hill, 1990).

In the case of Chile, the low volume of foreign investments in those export manufactures that are not linked to the country's natural resource base may stem not so much from any particular intrinsic aspects of such investments themselves but rather from a combination of other factors. An important element has of course been the relative availability of resources in Chile, a country where natural resources predominate and human capital is relatively scarce. This situation facilitates the attraction of external resources toward sectors related to natural resources, and it hampers the attraction of investments toward more sophisticated manufactures.

In addition, Chile's economic policy, with its predilection for flat incentives, has not given priority to the acquisition of new comparative advantages. In the only instance in which national policy has deviated from absolute neutrality in incentives (the debt conversion program), investments were channeled toward sectors with more complex technologies, thereby helping to establish Chile's presence in relatively new export markets. The overall impact of these policies can be evaluated as positive, because the investments in those higher-technology sectors have continued even after the termination of the subsidy implicit in the debt conversion program.

Technological Contribution of FDI

In analyzing the impact of FDI on the technological capability of Chile's economy, we shall base our observations on the survey results. The survey measured the technological contribution in various dimensions, as follows: (1) training of the national labor force; (2) expenditures in quality control; (3) introduction of products and production processes to the Chilean economy; (4) degree of innovation that FDI enterprises apply in Chile compared to the degree of innovation that they apply in other host countries; and (5) dissemination of technology into the Chilean economy by domestically subcontracting inputs or components locally produced to company specifications.

In general, the research results have not been encouraging. The interviewed FDI companies carry out some activities with positive technological externalities (training of the local work force or introduction of some technology that may be imitated by other companies), but they apparently have made very little effort thus far to transfer technologies or to create new ones. This may be the result of the sectoral distribution of FDI, since most FDI has been oriented toward sectors in which the pertinent technology is fairly standardized.

There are a few exceptions: the firms in the cellulose sector have undeniably introduced technologies new to the Chilean milieu. In effect, a significant portion of the capital brought into the cellulose sector by foreign enterprises (which have affiliated themselves with domestic enterprises) was in the form of technology (allowing the sector to employ, in many cases, international "best practices" in cellulose production). In the financial services sector there are indications that foreign investors have introduced technologies new to the local financial services arena.

Furthermore, all of the surveyed firms are extremely committed to training their local human resources[10] and to the applying quality control to the inputs they use. Most use imported technologies, but frequent efforts are made to adapt these technologies to the Chilean setting. A significant number of the interviewed firms associated themselves with similar local firms and increased their production capacity, helping, to some degree, to improve their production processes (although some of the interviewed executives stated that these advances were made independently of the presence of foreign capital).

Very few of the companies have made technological innovations in Chile. Instead, the processes they use and the products they introduce into Chile have tended largely to be adaptations and improvements of products or processes al-

---

[10] It should be pointed out, however, that Chile has a mechanism to subsidize labor training. In general, the large enterprises make use of this tax-based incentive.

ready existing in the investing firms' parent enterprises (or in another branch). Even so, in a few cases subsidiaries have indeed introduced technological and administrative innovations. FDI companies have not hesitated to subcontract on the local market, perhaps thereby contributing to the dissemination of foreign technologies—although it is difficult to say to what degree.

Conclusions and Policy Evaluation

The significant increase of FDI in Chile beginning in the 1986–87 period resulted from a series of factors, no single one of which was a sufficient cause in and of itself. As has been the case since the past century, abundant high-quality natural resources continue to be the major underlying "locational advantage" offered by Chile to FDI. The changes made in the country's legislation on FDI during the 1970s, which were very favorable to foreign enterprises, set the stage for the large increase in FDI (following a significant lag period) during the 1980s. When Chile began to correct the internal and external imbalances that had characterized its economy during the early 1980s, foreign investment began to flow into the country.

In the case of Chile, unlike the Argentine experience, privatizations did not play an important role in attracting foreign capital.[11] On the other hand, external debt capitalization had an important role. In the early stages, the implicit subsidy contained in the debt conversion program (Chapter XIX) was important in that it drew potential investors' attention to Chile. Later, FDI inflows no longer needed this support from public policy, and in fact we can now speak in terms of important structural change in regard to FDI volumes: the FDI-to-GDP ratio has climbed from a level of less than 1 percent during the first half of the 1980s to a current level of approximately 5 percent. The achievement of a fair degree of macroeconomic stability, perceived by investors as sustainable, clearly contributes to the maintenance of FDI inflows that are much larger than in the past, both in nominal magnitude and in relation to the total size of the Chilean economy. In this sense, the external debt conversion mechanism can be said to have been successful in that it was able to effectively turn around what had been the severest negative shock (the drying up of foreign capital as a result of the debt crisis) experienced by the Chilean economy since the Great Depression.

---

[11] During the period under analysis, no privatizations took place using foreign capital. One of the period's significant investments was the transfer of shares of the *Compañía de Teléfonos de Chile* from one foreign investor to another, but the purchase did not constitute a privatization. In general, the domestic private sector was the purchaser of most of the state-owned enterprises privatized in Chile during the 1980s.

With regard to FDI's impact on development, it can be said to have contributed to physical capital formation. Econometrically, there can be observed a positive relationship between FDI and total investment. Furthermore, the survey showed that the initial investment made by foreign firms is often merely a starting point. Usually there are expansions and further investments within a short while, both when FDI goes into purchase of existing assets and when it is used to create new projects.

Foreign direct investment has also contributed to the growth and diversification of exports, in part because much FDI has naturally flowed of its own accord into the export sector, and in part because Chilean economic policy (real devaluations and the creation of an implicit subsidy to foreign investment in favored sectors) has intentionally oriented FDI toward the export sector. The real possibility that the Chapter XIX program was used as an industrial policy tool, consciously or unconsciously, is suggested by two observations: first, the mode of FDI approval in each case and, second, the sectoral composition of the investments made via Chapter XIX (strongly oriented toward processed natural resources and toward financial services—an orientation significantly different from that of the FDI made through DL 600, a great deal of which flowed into the mining sector). These industrial promotion policies may also be evaluated as having been positive, since they constituted a decisive tool in bringing about the export diversification observed in recent years.

Chile's experience with Chapter XIX suggests several important economic policy conclusions. On the one hand, it has become apparent that with a set of simple rules (which, in the case of Chapter XIX, included clear criteria for FDI project approval, rapid approval, and limitations on its use in mining, which is Chile's sector of traditional comparative advantages), incentives can be effective in attracting significant volumes of foreign resources and in orienting them toward specific sectors. On the other hand, it has also become apparent that in the context of an open economy, it is not easy to orient foreign investments toward sectors in which the country does not possess clear comparative advantages. Chile's abundance of natural resources makes it inevitable that the country will attract natural resource-related investments. Until Chile improves the quality of its human resources and its economic and scientific infrastructure, it will not find it easy to attract investments toward sectors not related to the country's natural resource base.

Our final observation is that FDI's technological impact has not yet been of great significance. Although FDI has entailed a certain degree of technology transfer, that investment's sectoral composition (strongly concentrated in sectors employing internationally standardized technologies) has militated against the fulfillment of the objective that FDI ideally should entail a significant technological component. Apparently, a policy is needed that will—without abandoning Chile's essentially liberal-minded approach to FDI—assign priority to the transfer of technology and to encouraging national and foreign firms to carry out research and development activities in Chile. In order to create the proper framework, serious attention must be given to improving the country's human resource base (through thorough educational reform) and to promoting general scientific and technological activity.

Bibliography

Agosin, M.R., and F.J. Prieto. 1993. Trade and Foreign Direct Investment Policies: Pieces of a New Strategic Approach to Development? *Transnational Corporations* 2(2). New York: United Nations.

Agosin, M.R., R. Fuentes, and L. Letelier. 1994. Los capitales extranjeros en las economías latinoamericanas: el caso de Chile. In *Los capitales extranjeros en las economías latinoamericanas*, ed. J.A. Ocampo. Bogota: Inter-American Development Bank and FEDESARROLLO.

Ariff, M., and H. Hill. 1990. *Export-oriented Industrialization: The ASEAN Experience*. London: Allen and Urwin.

Desormeaux, J. 1989. *La inversión extranjera y su rol en el desarrollo de Chile*. Working Paper No. 119 (July). Instituto de Economía, Pontificia Universidad Católica de Chile, Santiago.

Economic Commission for Latin America and the Caribbean (ECLAC). 1990. *Conversión de la deuda externa en inversión: guía para el personal directivo*. LC/L. 595 (October). Santiago: ECLAC.

Ffrench-Davis, R. 1990. Debt-equity Swaps in Chile. *Cambridge Journal of Economics* 14 (March).

General Agreement on Tariffs and Trade (GATT). 1991. *Trade Policy Review - Thailand* 1. Geneva.

Ocampo, J.A., ed.. 1994. *Los capitales extranjeros en las economías latinoamericanas*. Bogota: Inter-American Development Bank and FEDESARROLLO.

Ozawa, T. 1992. Foreign Direct Investment and Economic Development. *Transnational Corporations* 1 (1). New York: United Nations.

Ros, J. 1994. Mercados financieros y flujos de capital en México. In J.A. Ocampo, ed., *op. cit.*

Rozas, P. 1992. *Inversión extranjera y empresas transnacionales en la economía de Chile (1974–89)*. Estudios e Informes de la CEPAL (No. 5, August). Santiago.

Annex: Variables for Applying the Empirical Analysis

Chilean consumer price index (CPI): series published in the BM (1989=100).

Country risk indicator (CR): external debt as a proportion of exports of goods and services. Figures from the BM.

Foreign direct investment (FDI): defined in the text.

Foreign price index (FPI): there exist two estimations, one with and one without Latin America. The series utilized is the first one (1986=100), *Monthly Bulletin*.

General real share price index [GRSPI](IGPAR): obtained from the Chilean Central Bank's *Boletín mensual* (BM) [Monthly Bulletin].

Gross domestic product (GDP): obtained directly from the BM and expressed in millions of 1977 pesos.

GDP variance (VARGDP): is the annual "movable" variance in GDP. This measure should capture the existence of stability in GDP growth—an important signal to FDI.

Inflation (INF): variation of the Chilean consumer price index.

Inflation variance (VARIN): this variable has a purpose similar to that of VARGDP, as a measure of internal economic stability.

Nominal exchange rate (NER): the measure is pesos per dollar, and the quarterly value is the average of the published monthly values of the BM.

Real exchange rate (RER): this is the nominal exchange rate deflated by the Chilean consumer price index and multiplied by the U.S. wholesale price index.

Real foreign direct investment (RFDI): expressed in millions of 1989 pesos, with nominal values deflated by the foreign price index.

Real FDI in dollars (FDI*): this is FDI in current dollars (from the BM and the Foreign Investment Committee), deflated by the U.S. wholesale price index.

Real GDP in dollars (Y*): this is current price GDP, converted to current dollars and deflated by the U.S. wholesale price index. Figures from the BM.

Tobin's Q (Q/Q): this indicator results from dividing the general nominal share price index by the wholesale price index, and the quarterly value is the average of the monthly values. The general nominal share price series and the wholesale price index series are published in the BM.

Total investment (TI): These figures, published in the BM, are available only in yearly form; thus, the series utilized in the regressions is a "quarterization." The figures are expressed in millions of 1977 pesos.

U.S. wholesale price index (USWPI): series published in the Central Bank's *Informe económico y financiero* (Economic and Financial Report) (1986=100).

F21, 016

137-78

CHAPTER FOUR

CHARACTERISTICS, DETERMINANTS AND EFFECTS OF FOREIGN DIRECT INVESTMENT IN COLOMBIA*

Roberto Steiner
Ursula Giedion

The 1990s have witnessed a significant inflow of international capital into Latin America, including a surge in foreign direct investment (FDI). Colombia has been among the recipients of these new capital inflows, though not to the same extent as many other countries of the region.

Evidence suggests that this recent flow of resources toward Latin America has been related in part to a slump in investment opportunities in the developed countries. Yet certain specific factors within each recipient Latin American country have also played a role in attracting the capital. The first two sections of this chapter examine the causality of such factors in terms of Colombia's official laws and regulations on FDI and in terms of reforms carried out in the economic arena; the first section provides a long-term analysis (1970–93), and the second section focuses in greater detail on more recent developments.

The third section describes and analyzes a survey of several companies in Colombia whose capital structure includes a significant FDI component. This survey made it possible for us to describe and define these companies, to pinpoint those elements that motivated the associated FDI, and to assess the companies' contribution to development and technology transfer. The transfer of technology is of crucial importance in that FDI's merits are related not only to its contribution to the balance of payments and to strengthening domestic savings, but also to its role as an intermediary between economic activity in Colombia and the development of technology elsewhere.

* The authors would like to acknowledge the collaboration of Jesús Alberto Cantillo, Christina Fernández, and Mariela Tamayo, with very special thanks to Martin Maurer. We would also like to express our appreciation to Manuel Agosin, Daniel Chudnovsky, Alberto Melo, Jaime Vatter, Jorge Sapoznikow, and the FEDESARROLLO seminar attendees for their comments.

Foreign Direct Investment, 1970–93

Official Regulatory Regimen[1]

With respect to Colombian laws on FDI, three distinct subperiods can be discerned. The first dates from enactment of the exchange rate statute (Decree Law 444 of 1967) through the beginning of the 1980s. The second period covers the 1980s; its principal feature was the application of Decision 220 of the Board of the Cartagena Agreement (JUNAC) in 1987. The third period comprises the FDI regimen in effect since 1991.

The FDI legislation enacted during the first period reflects the country's concern about the possible negative effects of foreign investment on balance of payments and a fear that it might replace domestic capital; it also reflects Colombia's desire to "channel" and plan foreign investment in accordance with the country's needs. The 1980s constituted a transitional stage involving the gradual elimination of restrictions on FDI. The advantages of foreign investment began to take on greater weight (especially relating to technology transfer) at a time when access to external credit was difficult and there was a worldwide trend toward economic liberalization and the opening up of countries' economies. This liberalization process was greatly stimulated by regional and international processes, such as the Uruguay Round of GATT beginning in 1986, the many national economic adjustment programs arrived at in conjunction with the International Monetary Fund (IMF), and the negotiations carried out within the framework of the Andean Pact.

This transition introduced various changes in FDI legislation, leading eventually to total liberalization after 1991. As a logical consequence of the transition, a body of laws was enacted that eliminated all restrictions and promoted foreign investment.

The "Directorial" Period (1967–80)[2]

Decree Law 444 of 1967 marked the beginning of a long period of restrictions on foreign investment. Although foreign investment's importance as a complement to savings and as a technology transfer mechanism was duly recognized, it was believed that such investment could have negative effects on the balance of payments (Mora, 1984), and that the country might benefit by channeling and controlling foreign investment in accordance with its needs. Thus, the National Planning Office (DNP) was designated the authority to govern foreign investment.

---

[1] This subsection is based on several issues of *Legislación económica*.
[2] For a detailed analysis, see Banco de la República (1987).

Numerous bureaucratic procedures were introduced for the authorization of the DNP and the conferral of rights to remit and reinvest profits and to repatriate capital. All applications had to be submitted to the National Planning Office for evaluation in accord with newly established criteria of analysis and approval. Preferential treatment was recommended for investment leading to export increases or export diversification, and there was a mandatory evaluation of the effect on employment generation and the balance of payments. It was also stipulated that the National Council on Economic and Social Policy (CONPES) should be empowered to impose more criteria "in order to ensure that the proposed foreign investment harmonized with the country's economic and social development programs and with the advisability of linking foreign capital to certain activities." (Garay and Pizano [1979] contains a detailed analysis of the evolution of the criteria used in granting authorizations.) Later, certain actual sectoral prohibitions were introduced. In order to limit FDI's effect on the balance of payments, profit remittance was limited to 10 percent of the registered capital, and the repatriation of capital was limited to the value of what the investor had imported, with no repatriation allowed on value increases. Furthermore, the payment of royalties was subject to official approval.

This "directorial" approach was reinforced by the 1973 incorporation of the JUNAC Decision 24 into national legislation six years later (as Decree 1900 of 1973). In order to enjoy the market liberalization benefits made possible by the Andean Pact, FDI-based companies would now first have to be converted into "mixed" companies. Apparently, however, this incentive was not sufficient to persuade existing companies to sign contracts for converting to mixed enterprises (Garay and Pizano, 1979). Although the ceiling on profit remittances was raised to 14 percent, foreign investors could not accumulate drawing rights or access domestic credit. In addition, regulations were enacted that limited transfer of foreign exchange abroad (for instance, a prohibition on the payment of royalties between affiliates and parent companies), thereby stimulating the use of alternative mechanisms for making payments abroad.

This 1967–80 subperiod was noteworthy for the absence of sectoral priorities. Although FDI was prohibited in certain sectors, there were no formal rules on sectoral preferences. The National Planning Office was authorized to approve or reject applications on the basis of the expected impact on national development. These criteria do not appear to have functioned to the benefit of any specific economic sectors.

The Transition: the 1980s

The debt crisis brought about a rethinking regarding the intrinsic value of foreign investment. Its traditional positive aspects, such as technology transfer and domestic savings complementation, once again surged to the forefront. To foster this strategy, the government simplified the bureaucratic procedures governing foreign direct investment and the associated profit remittances and capital repatriations. This did not go uncriticized by certain analysts (Mora, 1984).

In 1987, JUNAC issued Decision 220, which became the hallmark of this period. Decision 220 was noteworthy for the freedom it accorded to countries in their treatment of FDI. In this sense, it extended the time limit for conversion, and allowed full discretion regarding access to domestic credit and setting official ceilings on profit remittances. The government of Colombia made use of this margin of action to reduce restrictions in all areas. It raised the profit remittance ceiling to 25 percent, eliminated the conversion requirement, liberalized access to the domestic credit market (except for development credit), and authorized payment of royalties to the parent companies in the case of new technologies or technologies used for the production of export goods. Nevertheless, certain restrictions continued to exist, such as sectoral prohibitions—particularly in the financial sector.

The dismantling of legislation on FDI was initiated during a period of difficult access to external credit (Guisinger, 1986). A motivating role was also played by the global changes in development strategies such as market liberalization. The openness to foreign capital came into existence at a time when laws were changing all over the world in favor of foreign investment (UN, 1993).

Liberalization of FDI Treatment

The benchmark change toward FDI liberalization in Colombia was introduced in the form of JUNAC Decision 291, which was incorporated into the national body of laws through CONPES Resolution 49 of 1991, also known as the statute on international investments. For the first time, a single statute incorporated all of Colombia's existing regulations on FDI (including the special regimens for the financial sector and the petroleum/mining sector), a step that reflected a desire for greater transparency and clarity. More important than the specific legal provisions were the underlying principles upon which these provisions were based—namely, equality of treatment to national and foreign investors; universality of access to economic sectors; and automaticity of approval.

Included for the first time were explicit incentives to foreign investors (such as access to external credit lines and to export promotion mechanisms) on the same terms as those accorded to domestic investors. Nevertheless, the existing special regulations were retained for the financial services sector[3] and the petroleum/mining sector.[4]

---

[3] Any desired portion of a financial services sector enterprise's total shares could legally be held by a foreign investor, following authorization by the Banking Superintendency.

[4] The reintegration of the product from oil exports remains optional. National Planning Office authorization is no longer needed for mining sector FDI projects valued at less than $100 million.

CONPES Resolution 49 of 1991 was complemented and strengthened in December of that same year by Resolution 51, which eliminated further obstacles, in accordance with the spirit of the principles mentioned earlier. The ceiling on profit remittances abroad was eliminated, and the concept of what is meant by foreign investment was expanded to include indirect and portfolio investment and all of a company's in-kind capital contributions, including intangibles such as technological contributions, trademarks and patents. In addition, in order to make profit remittances, prior approval by the pertinent oversight bodies no longer had to be sought. Resolution 51 constitutes the international investments statute currently in force. Its major components include:[5]

•   *Equality of Treatment.* Except in the case of tax matters related to the transfer of resources abroad (which are governed by the Tax Statute and its attendant regulations), foreign investors may not be subjected to conditions different from those accorded to national investors.

•   *Universality.* Foreign investment is permitted in all of Colombia's economic sectors, except defense, national security, and the processing and disposal of toxic waste.

•   *Automaticity.* For purposes of attracting a larger quantity of foreign capital, most investment projects are no longer subject to prior approval by the National Planning Office. Nevertheless, authorization is still required in several sectors, including public services; the processing and disposal of waste matter; the hydrocarbons/mining sector when the project is valued at more than $100 million, except projects for hydrocarbon exploration and exploitation; and investment activities or insurance activities covered by any of eight international conventions ratified by Colombia, when so stipulated by the respective convention. Tacit administrative approval can be assumed to exist if the National Planning Office makes no pronouncement within 45 working days.

Resolution 51 confirmed the government's desire, as expressed in the earlier statute, to assume an active role in promoting foreign investment. The resolution stipulates that CONPES "will establish the guidelines for the development and implementation of a program designed to promote foreign investment...and to channel greater inflows of capital from abroad into the country." In keeping with this spirit, a specialized body, COINVERTIR, was created in 1992 for the specific purpose of promoting foreign investment in Colombia (DNP, 1993).

The Financial and Petroleum/Mining Sectors

Two sectors have always received special treatment with regard to foreign investment: the financial sector and the petroleum/mining sector. JUNAC Deci-

---

[5] See Buitrago (1991).

sion 24 prohibited FDI in the financial sector. Colombia, however, chose to focus on Article 44 of that decision, which stated that the recipient country was at liberty to apply sectoral prohibitions.[6] This approach permitted the absence of restrictions on foreign participation in the sector through 1975, when the banking sector was "Colombianized" through Law 55. This law, in effect until 1989, prohibited new foreign investment in the sector and required that already-established FDI financial firms convert into mixed enterprises.

The 1980s ushered in a change of attitude toward foreign investment, but the financial sector continued to be governed by Law 55. In those years the financial system underwent one of the most severe crises in its history, which implied an atmosphere more conducive to controlling the sector than to introducing modifications to its foreign investment laws. These laws, in fact, were not modified until the 1990s. In December 1990, Law 45 introduced a significant reform of the financial system, including new rules on capital amounts; greater flexibility in operational time terms; the strengthening of oversight and control mechanisms; and an expansion of financial service companies' possibilities. Law 45 allowed foreigners to own any portion of financial institutions' capital (García, 1992). The international investments statute currently in force in Colombia (Resolution 51 of 1991) contains the regimen applicable to foreign investment in the sector. This regimen allows nearly total freedom and equal treatment for foreign and national investors.

Colombia's petroleum/mining sector is governed by the International Investments Statute, the Petroleum Code and the Mining Code. The Ministry of Mines and Energy approves investment projects in petroleum and natural gas exploration and exploitation, once the foreign investor has negotiated the contract with the government's Colombian Petroleum Enterprise (ECOPETROL). The same ministry is also entrusted with authorizing investments in refinancing, transport and distribution, as well as in exploration, exploitation, smelting or transformation projects. Approval by the National Planning Office is required when the proposed investment is valued at more than $100 million.

The present system of foreign participation in the petroleum sector is one of association rather than concession (Cock, 1990). This system was introduced in Colombia in 1964, legally adopted in 1969, and established as the only legal form of contract beginning in 1974. The terms of such contracts and the way in which profits were divided between the state and the associated investment enterprise (foreign or national) have been severely criticized, because the

[6] Furthermore, the interpretation of Decision 24 allowed for a certain margin of freedom with respect to the regulations introduced. Thus, foreign participation greater than 49 percent was authorized if it was a question of avoiding the potential imminent failure of the financial institution. See *Banca y Finanzas* (1988 and 1989).

government's profit share is one of the highest in the world (between 81.8 percent and 85 percent).[7] Moreover, taxes are levied on the value of production, and not on profits. Furthermore, in 1989 it was decreed that an associate's participation would decrease with every discovery of an oil field with a cumulative production estimated at more than 60 million barrels. This trend is worrisome, given that Colombia has comparative advantages in oil production. It is gratifying, therefore, to note that measures have been announced that will change the situation: a reform of the contract regimen has been proposed in order to link contracts to profitability and not to the scale of production.

Laws on Taxation and the Exchange Rate—Complementary Considerations

If we were to consider only those laws directly addressing foreign investment, then we would be neglecting to analyze other important elements. A decision to invest involves considerations on the relative merit (compared with other countries) of laws on taxation and exchange rates. Clearly, it is beyond the scope of this study to examine all of the pertinent aspects and then to compare them with other countries at a similar developmental level. We can, however, at least mention the principal aspects of the respective Colombian laws in order to facilitate an analysis of present foreign investment and its outlook. Colombia's most important FDI-related tax provisions are the following (ECLAC, 1992; Ministerio de Hacienda, 1993):

•   Foreign enterprises and their branches are subject to taxes only on income generated in Colombia as profits and royalties and from provision of technical services and technical know-how. Income tax for foreigners and nationals alike has been standardized at 30 percent. A special 7.5 percent contribution has been established for the 1993–97 period, applicable to all those declaring income.

•   In the case of profits obtained through branches and other instances in which foreigners receive income while in Colombia, a remittance tax applies, complementary to the income tax, once the income tax has been deducted. This remittance tax is gradually decreasing, going from 12 percent in 1993 to 7 percent from 1996 onward. The remittance tax is different when there is reinvestment; if the reinvestment is maintained for 10 or more years, no such tax applies.

---

[7] Furthermore, as a result of the recent tax reform (Law 6 of 1992), the export of petroleum was taxed at a rate of $6 per barrel of light crude and $3.50 per barrel of heavy crude. On top of this was added a special contribution equal to 25 percent of the companies' income tax, as well as a remittance tax of 15 percent through 1995 and 12 percent thereafter.

- These taxes do not apply to income derived from hydrocarbon exploration and exploitation. In this area, a remittance tax of 15 percent from 1993 through 1995 and 12 percent from 1996 onward is applied. Furthermore, until 1997 a special contribution is applied equal to 25 percent of the taxpayer's income tax.

- A value-added tax applies to retail sales, imports and most services. The rate is 14 percent, although in some cases, such as exports, a zero percent rate may apply.

In general, it can be said that in comparison with other Latin American countries, Colombia's maximum tax rate of 30 percent applied to persons and companies is lower than the Latin American average of 35.4 percent for persons and 36.3 percent for companies (Tenjo, 1992). The profit remittance tax rate (12 percent in 1993) is higher than the Latin American average (10.6 percent in 1990).

With respect to exchange rate regulations, important changes have recently been introduced. Law 9 of 1991 superseded the previous exchange rate regimen (Decree Law 444 of 1967). The new regimen has made exchange rate control more flexible and has also reduced administrative intervention, decentralized operations and controls, granted greater space to the private financial system, and facilitated foreign investment, putting foreigners on an equal footing with nationals (Banco de la República, 1992).

In short, we can say that Colombia's exchange rate laws, like laws on taxation and FDI, have recently undergone significant streamlining and adaptation processes. But to assess the impact of such laws on potential investors in Colombia, it would be necessary first to carry out a highly detailed study of Colombia's differences in this area compared to other countries at a similar level of economic development.

Quantitative Aspects

Information Sources

In Colombia, foreign direct investment has been defined in Resolution 51 of 1991, in keeping with JUNAC Decision 291, as being all "contributions to an enterprise's capital that come from outside the country and belong to foreign natural or juridical persons." Also considered as FDI is the acquisition—with the idea of retaining them—of stocks, shares or other such titles on the stock market.

There are various sources of data on FDI. Each source presents a different slant and reflects in some way the desire to control FDI, especially before 1991. The National Planning Office's registry of FDI project applications and approvals constitutes an early data base, of interest especially if one wishes to analyze government policy on FDI during the period in which Decision 24 was in effect, because it reflects the criteria used to determine acceptance or rejection. This data base has its drawbacks, including disparities between investments approved and investments carried out, as well as lags between approval and project implementation. Furthermore, because of the 1991 changes in FDI laws, the continuity of this data series is not ensured.

For the purpose of controlling all foreign exchange flows associated with FDI, "all investments of capital from abroad, including the movement of additional investments, capitalizations, profit reinvestments with drawing rights, profit remittances, and capital reimbursements" had to be registered with the Banco de la República (BR). The BR series has good continuity, because the registration of these flows has always been obligatory. But this data source is nevertheless not free of defects: before 1979, the investor was not obliged to register the investment immediately but could instead wait and register it at the opportune moment for making capital or profit remittances. A large quantity of FDI was considered as "capital in limbo" (profit overruns vis-à-vis the official limits on profit transfers abroad) that was not registerable because it lacked drawing rights. Moreover, the registry included not only new FDI but also capitalizations and profit reinvestments, and did not include FDI in the petroleum sector.

A third data source consists of the FDI category in Colombia's balance of payments figures. Data in this category are arrived at by performing weighted calculations using FDI project approval figures from the National Planning Office and figures from the BR registry, bearing in mind the gaps and other data defects mentioned. The data cover the investments realized by means of imports of physical assets added to an enterprise's capital. They contain information on investments in petroleum and coal, obtained through surveys of enterprises in the sector (Banco de la República, 1989). There is no register by sectors or countries.

Bearing in mind the different limitations of each of these data sources, we have chosen to use the data from the BR registry, which provides a continuous and disaggregated data base. Since this source does not contain data on the petroleum sector, we also made use of balance of payments data, but these data cover only the years from 1980 onward.

Table 4.1 shows the FDI flow for the 1970–93 period, both with and without the petroleum and mining subsectors. Total investment reached its highest levels during the mid-1980s, by virtue of the events that occurred in the mining and petroleum sectors. Excluding those sectors, FDI has been stable, with a slight surge beginning in 1989, owing perhaps to the lifting of restrictions. Despite the recent favorable trend, the amounts continue to be low. With respect to gross fixed-capital formation, the flow without mining and petroleum ranged from the 1 percent level to the 4 percent level through 1985 and rose to around the 5 percent level in 1993.

Table 4.1. Summary of Foreign-Investment Flow in Colombia, 1970–93
(In current US$ millions)

	1970	1971	1972	1973	1974	1975	1976	1977	1978	1979	1980	1981
Total amounts												
With mines and petroleum[1]	105	44	39	20	24	48	53	116	43	113	122	188
Without mines and petroleum[1]	96	40	39	20	23	48	41	113	42	95	98	138
Importance of FDI in the economy												
Participation of total flow in the FBKF[2]	n.a.	3.3	2.8	1.3	1.2	2.4	2.2	4.1	1.2	2.6	2.2	3.0
Participation of total flow, without mines and petroleum, in the FBKF[2]	n.a.	2.9	2.8	1.3	1.1	2.4	1.7	4.0	1.2	2.2	1.8	2.2
Sectoral distribution (%)												
Primary sector	9.7	9.8	1.8	3.0	6.1	2.4	23.5	2.4	2.4	17.2	21.4	27.4
Agriculture, hunting, forestry and fishing	1.2	0.0	1.7	3.0	1.9	1.2	1.7	0.1	0.1	1.2	1.8	0.6
Exploitation of mines and quarries	8.5	9.8	0.1	0.0	4.2	1.2	21.9	2.3	2.3	15.9	4.5	1.1
Petroleum[3]	n.a.	n.a.	n.a.	n.a.	n.a.	n.a.	n.a.	n.a.	n.a.	n.a.	15.2	25.6
Secondary sector	2.7	64.5	70.7	49.6	50.2	66.0	50.3	75.3	74.0	67.2	82.7	62.9
Tertiary sector	17.3	24.6	26.8	43.3	43.3	31.6	26.3	22.1	23.5	15.3	-4.3	9.7
Unspecified activities	0.3	1.1	0.7	1.9	0.4	0.1	-0.1	0.1	0.1	0.3	0.2	0.1

Table 4.1 (cont.)

	1982	1983	1984	1985	1986	1987	1988	1989	1990	1991	1992	1993
Total amounts												
With mines and petroleum[1]	147	313	417	1.160	886	546	184	619	500	366	729	750
Without mines and petroleum[1]	61	106	134	49	69	-4	16	158	182	145	214	386
Importance of FDI in the economy												
Participation of total flow in the FBKF[2]	2.2	4.8	6.6	19.6	14.6	8.8	2.5	8.7	7.5	6.1	10.8	9.0
Participation of total flow, without mine and petroleum, in the FBKF[2]	0.9	1.5	2.1	0.8	1.1	-0.1	0.2	2.2	2.7	2.4	3.8	4.7
Sectoral distribution (%)												
Primary sector	58.4	66.7	67.3	95.9	92.3	101.4	91.1	74.5	64.7	60.9	71.4	50.1
Agriculture, hunting, forestry, and fishing	-0.3	0.5	-0.7	0.1	0.1	0.6	0.0	0.1	1.1	0.4	0.7	1.7
Exploitation of mines and quarries	35.8	3.4	42.2	38.0	42.0	59.5	1.1	16.3	9.7	-11.7	10.4	0.8
Petroleum[3]	22.9	62.6	25.7	57.8	50.2	41.3	90.0	58.1	53.9	72.2	60.3	47.6
Secondary sector	36.6	22.0	26.4	2.2	8.3	-2.0	15.2	24.3	23.6	36.1	9.6	26.4
Tertiary sector	5.0	10.3	7.1	1.9	-0.6	0.6	-6.3	1.2	11.7	3.0	18.9	23.1
Unspecified activities	—	1.0	-0.8	—	—	—	—	—	—	0.1	0.1	0.4

Sources: Banco de la República and author calculations.
[1] For 1970-79 no data exist on investment flows in the petroleum subsector.
[2] Gross fixed-capital formation.
[3] Data on petroleum according to balance-of-payments information.

Table 4.2 shows that the amount or stock of FDI in Colombia, without the mining sector,[8] was $2.705 billion in 1993, representing 5.5 percent of GDP. If the mining sector is included, the ratio jumps to 8.8 percent. The FDI share of the secondary sector (mostly manufactures) is higher than that of the other sectors for almost the entire period and then declines from 1984, when investment in the mining sector increased, because of the large coal and nickel exploitation projects (Cerrejón Norte and Cerromatoso).

An analysis of the flow of FDI enables us to visualize in greater detail the evolution of the three main sectors, including the petroleum sector. The great importance of foreign investment in the primary sector is immediately apparent—a scenario dominated by the mining and petroleum sectors. In 1985, investment in petroleum accounted for 58 percent of the total flow, much more than the 38 percent investment in coal. After 1988, investment shares in the sector began to decline—a trend that will probably be reversed in the figures for 1994 onward because of the discovery of oil fields in El Casanare. The tertiary sector has been the most dynamic sector in recent years, thanks largely to the privatization of financial institutions.

Petroleum discoveries and the privatization of financial institutions have helped make FDI's sectoral distribution more balanced than it was 20 years ago: the secondary sector had accounted for 70 percent of the total stock in 1970, but only 44 percent in 1993, giving way to the primary sector (39 percent in 1993) and to the tertiary sector (18 percent). Despite the relative recuperation of FDI in the financial sector, no high-growth phases can be discerned for the total. The phases identified in the corresponding legislation are not significantly reflected in the quantitative evolution.

Table 4.3 and Table 4.4 show the flow and the amount of FDI by country and region of origin. The petroleum sector is not represented, because of a lack of data. During the period covered, FDI is strongly dominated by the United States, a trend that started to emerge strongly in the early 1980s. As in the case of sectoral structure, there have been no important changes in FDI's structure by country or region of origin. Nevertheless, two points should be given special note. First, the participation of other Latin American countries was never significant, despite the laws favorable to intra-Andean investment; the recent liberalization, more than the integration-related efforts of the past two decades, seems to be what has revitalized investment by other countries of Latin America. Second, FDI from financial centers always participated significantly—a fact that implies a possible overestimation of FDI, since much of the capital actually consists of Colombian "flight" capital.

---

[8] No data were available on FDI levels in the petroleum sector.

Summary

Up to 1990, despite a change in the laws from a "directorial" approach toward a liberalization policy, no major changes had occurred in FDI. No important increase was seen during the prior two decades, but instead, very stable patterns emerged. Only the investments in the petroleum/mining sector, during the 1980s, showed a significant increase in amounts and sectoral distribution. The modest upturn in foreign investment noted during the past several years is most probably a result, at least in part, of the new official FDI regimen. Still, it would be premature at this time to speak of a radical change. It is too early to determine whether these investments are the beginning of a new phase, or whether they represent an inflow of repressed investments that occurred when the new FDI regimen was implemented—in which case, the increase will be of short duration.

Recent Evolution of FDI

Recent years have witnessed an important inflow of capital into Latin America. The figures in Table 4.5 show that Colombia has shared in this process. The table suggests that through 1992 the increase in reserves stemmed from current account transactions, but several studies (cited in Ocampo and Steiner, 1994) indicate that this current account surplus was actually masking short-term financial transactions heretofore prohibited by Colombian law.

With respect to FDI, Table 4.6 shows that although foreign investment may not have been as dynamic in Colombia as in other countries,[9] it has nonetheless not been negligible. In effect, $3.332 billion out of the $4.453 billion increase in Colombia's foreign reserves between 1987 and 1993 can be explained by the behavior of net FDI. Given the low rates of Colombian investment in other countries, this figure is dominated by FDI into Colombia. In 1992 alone, net foreign investment reached the significant level of $740 million.

If, however, we exclude petroleum sector FDI from these figures, the scenario changes dramatically, in a way that tends to bolster the widespread belief that Colombia has not really actively participated in the recent surge of FDI toward Latin America.[10] In fact, in a recent ECLAC document (1993) that lists the 60 most important foreign enterprises in Latin America in 1991, the first nine such firms included only one petroleum company (six belonged to the automo-

---

[9] For the case of Argentina, see Fanelli and Damill (1994). The Chilean experience is described in Agosin *et al.* (1994), and the Mexican experience is covered by Ros (1994).

[10] The figures used in the preceding section and in the present one as well (except for the balance of payments figures in Table 4.6) refer to FDI registered during the period.

150

150

Table 4.2. Summary of the Amount of Foreign Investment in Colombia, 1970–93[1]

(In current US$ millions)

	1970	1971	1972	1973	1974	1975	1976	1977	1978	1979	1980	1981
Total amounts												
With mining	457	502	540	560	584	633	686	801	844	957	1,061	1,201
Without mining	448	488	527	547	570	618	659	772	814	909	1,007	1,145
Importance of FDI in the economy												
Participation of total flow in GDP	6.4	6.5	6.3	5.5	4.8	4.9	4.5	4.1	3.7	3.4	3.2	3.3
Participation of total flow, without mines, in GDP	6.3	6.3	6.1	5.4	4.7	4.8	4.3	4.0	3.5	3.3	3.1	3.2
Sectoral distribution (%)												
Primary sector	2.9	3.5	3.4	3.4	3.5	3.4	4.9	4.6	4.5	6.0	6.1	5.7
Agriculture, hunting, forestry, and fishing	0.9	0.8	0.9	1.0	1.0	1.0	1.1	0.9	0.9	0.9	1.1	1.0
Exploitation of mines and quarries	2.0	2.7	2.5	2.4	2.5	2.4	3.9	3.6	3.6	5.0	5.1	4.6
Secondary sector	69.4	69.0	69.1	68.4	67.7	67.5	66.2	67.5	67.8	67.8	70.7	72.3
Tertiary sector	27.5	27.2	27.2	27.9	28.5	28.7	28.5	27.6	27.4	26.0	22.9	21.8
Unspecified activities	0.2	0.3	0.3	0.4	0.4	0.4	0.3	0.3	0.3	0.3	0.3	0.3

Table 4.2. (cont.)

	1982	1983	1984	1985	1986	1987	1988	1989	1990	1991	1992	1993
Total amounts												
With mining	1,314	1,431	1,741	2,231	2,672	2,992	3,011	3,270	3,500	3,602	3,952	4,328
Without mining	1,206	1,312	1,446	1,495	1,564	1,560	1,576	1,734	1,916	2,061	2,336	2,705
Importance of FDI in the economy												
Participation of total flow in GDP	3.4	3.8	4.6	6.6	7.8	8.4	7.8	8.4	8.8	8.5	9.1	8.8
Participation of total flow, without mines, in GDP	3.1	3.5	3.9	4.4	4.6	4.4	4.1	4.4	4.8	4.9	6.5	5.5
Sectoral distribution (%)												
Primary sector	9.2	9.3	17.6	33.5	42.0	48.4	48.2	47.5	45.9	43.5	41.6	38.5
Agriculture, hunting, forestry, and fishing	0.9	1.0	0.6	0.6	0.5	0.6	0.6	0.5	0.6	0.7	0.7	1.0
Exploitation of mines and quarries	8.3	8.3	17.0	33.0	41.5	47.9	47.7	47.0	45.3	42.8	40.9	37.5
Secondary sector	70.1	69.2	63.2	50.5	44.9	39.7	40.4	41.8	42.4	44.9	42.7	43.6
Tertiary sector	20.5	21.0	19.0	15.8	13.0	11.7	11.3	10.6	11.6	11.5	15.6	17.8
Unspecified activities	0.2	0.4	0.2	0.1	0.1	0.1	0.1	0.1	0.1	0.1	0.1	0.2

Sources: Banco de la República and author calculations.
[1] Does not cover petroleum-related FDI, since data were unavailable on FDI levels in the petroleum subsector.

Table 4.3. Distribution of FDI Flows in Colombia by Region of Origin, 1970–93
(In current US$ millions)

Region of Origin	1970	1971	1972	1973	1974	1975	1976	1977	1978	1979	1980	1981
North America	53	22	16	7	10	15	19	73	20	58	76	85
Latin America	7	1	1	1	—	13	14	2	2	2	17	2
Financial centers	11	11	8	5	4	8	4	5	6	5	-1	13
Europe	33	11	11	8	8	12	14	31	14	48	10	39
Asia	—	—	2	—	2	—	2	5	—	1	1	—
Other countries	—	—	—	—	—	—	—	—	—	—	—	—
Total	105	44	39	20	24	48	53	116	43	113	104	140

Region of Origin	1982	1983	1984	1985	1986	1987	1988	1989	1990	1991	1992	1993
North America	59	54	229	449	356	415	-6	148	125	29	104	158
Latin America	4	7	-3	4	1	-7	-5	51	7	0	40	100
Financial centers	7	7	2	13	10	6	-1	19	43	6	113	110
Europe	43	49	61	17	71	-94	32	50	46	35	94	66
Asia	—	—	20	7	2	—	-1	-9	10	32	-1	2
Other countries	—	—	—	—	—	—	—	—	—	—	1	1
Total	115	117	310	490	441	321	18	259	230	102	350	436

Sources: Banco de la República and author calculations.
Note: Does not include FDI in petroleum.

Table 4.4. Distribution of FDI Amounts in Colombia by Region and Country of Origin, 1970–93
(*Percentages*)

Region/Country of Origin	1970	1971	1972	1973	1974	1975	1976	1977	1978	1979	1980	1981
North America	65.7	64.3	62.7	61.6	60.8	58.4	56.6	57.6	57.1	56.4	68.1	58.3
United States	52.9	51.6	50.8	50.0	49.7	48.1	49.4	54.0	53.5	53.0	54.1	54.6
South America	5.1	4.9	4.8	4.8	4.6	6.3	7.8	6.9	6.9	6.3	7.3	6.6
Venezuela	1.9	1.7	1.6	1.6	1.6	3.1	3.1	3.5	3.1	3.0	4.3	3.9
Financial centers	12.2	13.2	1.38	14.2	14.2	14.5	14.0	12.7	12.7	11.7	10.5	10.4
Panama	6.7	7.3	7.7	8.0	8.0	8.5	8.1	7.4	7.5	6.9	6.5	5.8
Europe	16.8	17.4	18.2	19.0	19.6	20.1	20.5	21.4	22.0	24.3	22.9	23.6
Other countries	0.3	0.2	0.6	0.5	0.8	0.8	1.0	1.4	1.4	1.3	1.3	1.1

Region/Country of Origin	1982	1983	1984	1985	1986	1987	1988	1989	1990	1991	1992	1993
North America	57.8	56.8	59.9	66.9	69.1	75.6	74.9	73.5	72.2	71.0	67.3	64.2
United States	54.2	53.4	56.2	64.1	66.9	73.5	72.7	71.8	70.6	79.2	65.5	62.5
South America	6.4	6.3	5.0	4.1	3.5	2.9	2.7	4.0	4.0	3.8	4.5	6.3
Venezuela	3.8	3.5	2.8	2.2	1.9	1.2	1.1	2.5	2.3	2.3	2.9	4.1
Financial centers	10.0	9.7	8.1	6.9	6.1	5.7	5.6	5.8	6.6	6.6	8.9	10.5
Panama	5.7	5.6	4.6	3.4	3.2	3.2	3.1	3.2	3.2	3.4	4.3	4.8
Europe	24.8	26.2	25.0	20.3	19.6	14.4	15.3	15.7	15.9	16.4	17.4	17.1
Other countries	1.1	1.0	2.0	1.8	1.6	1.5	1.4	1.1	1.3	2.1	1.9	1.8

Sources: Banco de la República and author calculations.
Note: Does not include FDI in petroleum.

154

Table 4.5. Colombia's Balance of Payments, 1987–93
(US$ millions)

	1987	1988	1989	1990	1991	1992	1993[a]
Current account	-20.6	-215.6	-201.0	543.4	2,346.6	964.8	-1,578.5
Capital account	-9.2	937.8	478.6	-1.3	-782.0	175.7	1,487.2
Net direct investment	287.1	158.4	547.1	484.1	432.6	740.0	682.3
Into Colombia	312.6	202.8	576.2	500.5	456.8	790.0	922.3
From Colombia	22.5	44.4	29.1	16.4	24.2	50.0	240.0
Errors, omissions, and balancing entries	2.0	-362.2	-220.7	92.3	354.4	461.7	0.0
Change in net reserves	-27.8	360.0	56.9	634.4	1,919.0	1,602.2	-91.3

Source: Banco de la República.
[a] Provisional.

Table 4.6. Foreign Direct Investment[a] 1987–93
(US$ millions)

	Total	Manufacturing industry	Financial services	Mines and quarries	Agriculture	Construction	Trade/ Commerce	Transport and communications	Other[b]
1987	320.6	-11.2	—	324.8	3.3	-4.7	6.4	1.9	0.1
1988	18.4	27.9	-3.0	2.1	0.0	-18.2	10.0	1.6	-2.0
1989	259.2	150.5	3.2	101.0	0.3	0.5	2.1	1.2	0.4
1990	230.2	118.0	4.8	48.3	5.3	41.7	12.1	0.0	0.0
1991	101.8	132.0	4.2	-42.8	1.5	-1.0	7.4	-0.3	0.8
1992	288.9	69.8	91.9	75.5	5.4	19.3	19.4	6.6	1.0
1993	392.9	197.9	115.6	6.0	12.9	19.0	31.2	5.8	4.3
Total	1,611.9	684.9	216.7	514.9	28.7	56.6	88.7	16.8	4.6

Source: Banco de la República.
[a] Excluding petroleum. SITC, revision 2.
[b] Electricity, natural gas, water services; communal, social, and personal services; services to companies; and other unspecified activities.

tive sector, one to the tobacco sector, one to the food sector, and one to the petro-leum sector). The only three Colombia-based FDI companies to make the top-60 list were petroleum sector companies.

In order to explain FDI's recent evolution in Colombia, it would be helpful to distinguish between FDI directed toward the petroleum/mining sector and FDI directed toward the rest of the economy. The figures in Table 4.6 show that from 1987 to 1993 there was $1.612 billion of nonpetroleum-related FDI; of that sum, some $515 million corresponded to the mining and quarries subsector. There-fore, if petroleum and mining are excluded, Colombia during that seven-year period received a total of $1.1 billion of FDI—a not altogether spectacular figure compared to many other Latin American countries' FDI receipts during the pe-riod, and certainly a far cry from Colombia's own 1968–87 experience, when FDI growth was higher in Colombia than in Brazil, Mexico and Argentina.[11] By any definition, the figures show that in more recent times, FDI in Colombia has not significantly shifted its focus and that as recently as the end of 1993, only 43 percent was in the manufacturing sector.

Let us briefly focus on the behavior of FDI directed toward the manufactur-ing sector. From Table 4.6 we can infer that manufacturing sector FDI accounted for 42 percent of the total (excluding petroleum) and 62 percent (excluding both petroleum and mining). The sector-by-sector data (Standard International Trade Classification, revision 2) are presented in Table 4.7. During the 1987–93 period, 34 percent of industrial or manufacturing FDI in Colombia went into the machin-ery and equipment sector, 36 percent into the chemicals sector, and 13 percent into the foods, beverages and tobacco sector. Industrial FDI averaged $98 mil-lion per year during the 1987–93 period, but in 1993 it was $198 million.

In general terms, our analysis of FDI during the most recent period yields the following basic conclusions:

•   Total FDI (including petroleum) has been on the order of $480 million per year—a significant amount, given the size of Colombia's world trade.
•   If petroleum subsector FDI is excluded, that average is significantly re-duced, to a little more than $230 million.
•   Although not spectacular, the levels reached in 1992 and 1993 suggest an upsurge in FDI, even though the country's level does remain relatively low com-pared to the rest of Latin America.

The increase of FDI in the region has been explained in part by factors re-lated to the investment climate in the developed economies related to a signifi-

---

[11] Brewer (1991) notes that in 1985, some 61 percent of total FDI was in the primary sector, while the respective figures for Argentina and Brazil were only 27.4 percent and 13.5 percent. In Mexico, by 1984, some 76 percent of FDI was going into the secondary sector.

Table 4.7. Foreign Direct Investment in the Manufacturing Industry, 1987–93
(US$ millions)

	Foods, beverages and tobacco	Textiles and leather	Wood	Paper	Chemicals	Nonmetallic minerals	Basic metals	Machinery and equipment
1987	9.4	0.5	0.4	5.5	22.3	3.7	1.0	-54.6
1988	14.6	1.8	0.5	4.9	8.8	2.3	0.3	-5.8
1989	20.0	1.4	-0.4	3.7	45.1	6.5	5.2	69.0
1990	-1.0	1.8	0.9	14.4	9.0	-0.9	-0.5	94.4
1991	18.9	6.3	0.0	8.3	27.9	2.8	-2.2	69.7
1992	6.1	5.7	0.2	2.3	28.8	5.8	6.2	13.7
1993	20.1	7.9	2.0	5.0	102.1	16.5	0.9	43.1
Total	88.1	25.4	3.6	44.1	244.0	36.7	10.9	229.5

Source: Banco de la República.

cant decline in capital yield rates, and in part by factors of attraction (related to a more propitious macroeconomic situation, privatizations and debt conversion programs). Colombia has not implemented a debt-conversion program; furthermore, the country's privatization efforts have been timid and not necessarily oriented toward foreign investment promotion. Finally, the main structural reforms have only recently been applied.

If we then factor in Colombia's current delicate situation in regard to the question of public order, stemming in part from the country's efforts to combat drug trafficking,[12] we can understand why FDI in Colombia has not increased dramatically in recent years. According to Brewer's (1991) indicators of stability, transparency and hospitality, as gleaned from his 11-country study of FDI recipients (including Argentina, Brazil, Colombia and Mexico), none presented a more adverse combination of indicators than Colombia.

Survey on Foreign Direct Investment

The survey was targeted at secondary sector and tertiary sector enterprises with foreign investment as part of their ownership structure. The survey's objective was to determine the profile of these enterprises, the factors that led them to invest in Colombia, and their contribution to Colombian development, principally through the transfer of technology.[13]

According to the information provided by the Superintendency of Corporations, as of late 1992 there were in Colombia some 403 business partnership enterprises with foreign participation in their capital. Based on these data, the survey sample was constructed. The survey excluded enterprises in the agricultural and petroleum/mining sectors. In addition, the following criteria were used: (i) 1992 value of assets greater than $2 million (which at late-1992 exchange rates meant about $2.7 million) and (ii) foreign capital participation of at least 25 percent. Of the 403 FDI enterprises mentioned, 152 fulfilled the requirements established for the construction of our sample.

---

[12] Political instability has been empirically identified as one factor that negatively affects FDI (Schneider and Frey, 1985), even though the variables used by these authors to approximate the concept of political instability (such as the amount of "soft" aid received from Soviet bloc countries) are far from adequate to reflect the type of instability that has recently affected Colombia. In Koechlin (1992) there are alternative definitions of political instability.

[13] Data disaggregations were made for the three sectors with the greatest participation in the total: (i) metalworking; (ii) chemicals, petroleum derivatives, rubber and plastic; and (iii) nonmetallic minerals.

Table 4.8. Percentage of Responses

International Standard Industrial Classification Number	# Enterprises	% Assets
30 Primary sector	n.a.	n.a.
31 Foods	31.3	51.4
32 Textiles	14.3	60.8
33 Wood	0.0	0.0
34 Paper	27.3	84.0
35 Chemicals	37.5	40.8
36 Nonmetallic minerals	60.0	85.3
38 Basic industries	41.2	58.1
39 Metalworking	25.0	22.7
40-50 Tertiary sector	27.8	22.0
Total for the industrial sector	34.9	54.8
Total	36.6	52.2

Source: FEDESARROLLO.

Representativeness of the Survey

An analysis of the survey's representativeness was carried out on the basis of the three following indicators: number of enterprises, total assets, and production.

Number of Enterprises

As shown in Table 4.8, 37 percent of the chosen 152 firms responded to the survey. This result is higher than the average response received by FEDESARROLLO to other special modules of business opinion surveys. At a disaggregated level, the best-represented sector is the sector producing nonmetallic mineral products (clay, china and porcelain objects, glass and other construction materials). The survey also drew a good response from the metalworking industry and the chemicals sector. The lowest index of representativeness (14 percent) was registered in the textile sector.

Total Assets

The assets of the responding enterprises constituted 52.2 percent of the assets belonging to all of the selected firms (Table 4.8). In accordance with this asset measure, the greatest representativeness is found in the nonmetallic minerals sector, reinforcing the result of the previously described indicator. In second place is the paper, cardboard and printing industry. Other sectors with high asset-based representativeness in the survey are textiles and basic metal products. The degree

Table 4.9. Representativeness of the Annual Survey of Manufacturers (EAM)
(1990 data)

SITC		Low range	High range
31	Foods	3.36	5.05
32	Textiles	3.78	5.20
33	Wood	0.0	0.0
34	Paper	15.53	22.08
35	Chemicals	10.96	19.93
36	Nonmetallic minerals	11.91	28.75
37	Basic industries	0.0	0.00
38	Metalworking	17.58	23.72
39	Other	5.59	11.18
Total		7.95	12.61

Sources: National Statistical Office (DANE) and author calculations.

of representativeness obtained from the analysis of assets is greater than the degree obtained from the point of view of number of responding enterprises; thus, the survey can provide information from the very largest firms from among all the firms to whom the survey was sent.

Production[14]

The production levels of the surveyed FDI enterprises were analyzed in relation to total production of all firms covered in the Annual Survey of Manufacturers, since there were no production figures for firms with foreign investment. The survey represented from 8 percent to 12.6 percent[15] of total manufacturing production (Table 4.9). At the sectoral level, the greatest representativeness is in nonmetallic minerals, metalworking, and the paper-related industries. The foregoing results indicate that the information obtained from the survey relates, for the most part, to sectors in which foreign investment's production is significant at the national level.

---

[14] The basis for performing the calculations was the response to the survey question about the responding firms' production level during the past five years.
[15] The high level of these estimates is biased downward, since it was assumed that firms with production equal to or greater than $Col 100,000 millions would produce only the $Col 100,000 millions.

Profile of the Responding Firms

Participation of Foreign Capital

In 85 percent of the cases, FDI accounts for more than 50 percent of the firm's ownership composition (Table 4.10). The concentration of foreign capital is particularly high in the chemical products sector, where 85 percent of the firms show FDI participation accounting for more than 75 percent of their ownership structure. This concentration of capital is consistent with the results of other studies. Echavarría and Esguerra (1990) found that of 252 enterprises in the manufacturing sector with some foreign investment, some 63.5 percent had foreign ownership participation greater than 50 percent.

The fact that the foreign investors in such firms are most often also important shareholders is related to the characteristics of the industrial branches in which FDI is concentrated: chemicals, paper-related products, metal products, rubber, the automotive industry, pharmaceuticals, and electric machinery. One ECLAC study shows that a shared feature of these sectors is their high rates of investment in technology (Misas, 1993).

It should be pointed out, however, that 36 percent of the surveyed enterprises have significant national participation (higher than 25 percent). This 36 percent of companies is found primarily in the metalworking and mineral products sectors, which produce goods with a relatively low technological content (for instance, paper production, glass products, container manufacturing, brick production) or which involve activities in which knowledge of the domestic market is a basic aspect (for instance, in distribution of television sets and printed matter). The companies with a 50 percent or higher national ownership participation indicated that they were not affiliated with any parent company. These cases thus involve foreigners who invest in Colombia on their own. It is possible that the lack of a parent company with experience in international marketing relationships accounts at least in part for the creation of jointly owned enterprises: the national partners, whose major advantage over the foreign partners is knowledge of the domestic market, may fill the vacuum created by the absence of a parent company.

Targeted Market

The domestic market is the primary sales target: 81 percent of companies directed more than 80 percent of 1992 company sales to the domestic market. Nevertheless, in recent years the export market has been gaining in importance (Table 4.11); in 1987, fully 56.6 percent of the firms had sold exclusively on the domestic market, whereas this proportion fell to 28.3 percent in 1992. Although these companies appear to be turning increasingly to the foreign market, the new mar-

Table 4.10. Participation by Foreign Capital

	National total	Chemical products	Nonmetallic minerals	Metalworking
TOTAL RESPONDING COMPANIES	53	18	6	14
By size:				
Less than 5 billion	14	4	1	5
Between 5 and 10 billion	10	2	1	3
Between 11 and 50 billion	19	10	3	4
More than 51 billion	10	2	1	2
Total	53	18	6	14
By market:				
Exporters	35	13	5	10
Non-exporters	18	5	1	4
Total	53	18	6	14
By investment origin:				
Purchase of a national company	10	4	2	3
Branch establishment	22	9	1	3
Joint venture	16	4	2	7
Establishment of a new company	5	1	1	1
Total	53	18	6	14
By capital participation:				
Less than 25%	—	—	—	—
Between 25% and 50%	8	2	1	4
Between 51% and 75%	11	1	2	3
Greater than 76%	34	15	3	7
Total	53	18	6	14
By sector:				
Manufactures	48	n.a.	n.a.	n.a.
Commerce/trade	3	n.a.	n.a.	n.a.
Services	2	n.a.	n.a.	n.a.
Total	53	n.a.	n.a.	n.a.

Source: FEDESARROLLO.

Table 4.11. Companies Directing Production to Domestic Market
(Percentage)

	100% of market	More than 80% of market
1987	56.6	83.0
1988	56.6	86.8
1989	54.7	83.0
1990	47.2	86.8
1991	37.7	83.0
1992	28.3	81.1

Source: FEDESARROLLO.

Table 4.12. Companies Directing Some Production to Latin American Market
(Percentage)

Percentage	1987	1988	1989	1990	1991	1992
0	69.8	66.0	64.2	56.6	—	35.8
1-10	20.8	24.5	22.6	30.2	37.7	43.4
11-20	5.7	5.7	5.7	7.5	5.7	5.7
21-30	3.8	3.8	7.5	5.7	9.4	11.3
31-40	—	—	—	—	1.9	3.8

Source: FEDESARROLLO.

kets are practically confined to Latin America (Table 4.12). No firm exports more than 10 percent of its production outside the region, and only 9.4 percent of these firms targeted up to 10 percent of their sales to other countries (on average) during the 1987–92 period (Table 4.13).

Size and Age of Firms

Some 93 percent of the enterprises are, in terms of assets, among the largest 1,000 companies in the country. In comparison with national firms, according to Echavarría and Esguerra (1990), the firms with foreign capital tend to be larger. In terms of their age, it is interesting to note that the great majority (86 percent) were established in Colombia before 1980. Although this result may be slightly skewed by the newer companies' relative disinclination to respond to the survey, it nevertheless corroborates certain earlier findings.[16] This information also con-

---

[16] According to Echavarría and Esguerra (1990), foreign enterprises are, on the average, older than domestic enterprises.

Table 4.13. Companies Directing Some Production to Markets outside Latin America
(Percentage)

Percentage	1987	1988	1989	1990	1991	1992
0	90.6	92.5	92.5	90.6	88.7	88.7
1-10	9.4	7.5	7.5	9.4	11.3	11.3
10-100	0	0	0	0	0	0

Source: FEDESARROLLO.

firms something that was stated earlier: no major increase in foreign investment has occurred in Colombia in recent years, either in terms of the amounts invested or the number of foreign enterprises entering the country.

Determinants of Foreign Direct Investment

The survey sought to rank those factors that led a firm to invest in Colombia: macroeconomic situation, trade policy, legal framework, microeconomic conditions, or the firm's global strategy. This last factor, which may seem to be somewhat imprecise, includes investment determinants related to access to different markets (domestic, Latin American, U.S. markets, and input markets as well). The firms were asked to rank these determinants, in order of importance.[17] In the following paragraphs we shall analyze the results of question 6 of Table 4.14 at the aggregate level and by sectors.

The most important determinant is the firm's overall strategy (Table 4.14, question 2). The second most important factor is Colombia's macroeconomic policy (question 1). A distant third place position was held by Colombia's treatment of foreign investment and trade policy (question 3). Microeconomic elements (question 5) were not considered very important at all. This finding held true at the sectoral level as well: for the three most important sectors, the firm's strategies and macroeconomic policy were again the main determinants.

Disaggregating the firm's overall or global strategy into its component parts (Table 4.14, question 2), the most important component was considered to be the prospects for access to the domestic market. Given the relatively small size of the Colombian market, it might be worthwhile to try to ascertain exactly what

---

[17] The factor considered most important received three points, the second most important factor received two points, the third most important factor received one point, and the other factors received no points. These results were totaled for the 56 responding firms. Then the sum of the points received for each possible factor was divided by the weighted total [56 (3+2+1) = 336].

Colombia's potential might be for attracting greater levels of foreign investment. It is interesting to note that in many of these sectors the potential for new foreign enterprises is small, since some of the world's largest transnational corporations already have branches in Colombia.

To these doubts about the potential of foreign investment in so far as it is oriented to the (limited) domestic market must be added the concern with economic liberalization, as foreign competition will also vie for a share of this domestic market. A recent unrelated FEDESARROLLO survey allows us to make some inferences about the competitive capacity of the firms presently operating in Colombia.

The unprecedented growth of imports into Colombia (50 percent between 1992 and 1993) could negatively affect the foreign firms if they are unprepared to meet the competition. Fear of such competition could lead not only to levelling of investment, but even to disinvestment by those companies that have thus far survived by dint of the protection of the domestic market. A survey taken between January 1993 and January 1994 (FEDESARROLLO, 1994) asked 455 enterprises (ranked by export level) about their concerns about liberalization. More than 14 percent of the interviewed companies have more than 25 percent foreign participation, which suggests that these survey results might be relevant to our present discussion.

The results of this survey also corroborate some statements made earlier (Table 4.15). To begin with, the survey confirms that the foreign companies do not focus on the export market: 55 percent of the foreign enterprises export less than 30 percent of their production, and 27 percent of them direct all of their production to the domestic market. Furthermore, 97 percent of the foreign firms have sales greater than $1 billion and therefore are considered as large or medium sized. With respect to liberalization, more than 12 percent of the foreign investors felt themselves to be excellently positioned and nearly 63 percent felt well positioned to face international competition; these percentages do not differ significantly from the results of the national aggregate. It is interesting to note that when we disaggregate by market, the large and small foreign exporters tend to fear liberalization more than do the national companies; some 25 percent of the large exporting FDI firms feel themselves to be only in a "fair" or "poor" position to confront international competition, while only 19 percent of national exporting firms share this view. In general, however, the foreign enterprises feel capable enough to face competition.

There does not seem to be much risk of a plateauing or a withdrawal of foreign investment following the market opening. It is also worth noting that the recent survey on opening up the economy showed that eventual partnership with a foreign investor does not occupy an important position within national firms' ranking of potential strategies for dealing with stiffer foreign competition.

Going back to the survey carried out for this chapter, a strategy that does

Table 4.14. Investment Determinants, According to Survey Responses
(Percentages)

Factors that Influenced the Investment Decision	Responses
1. Most important macroeconomic elements:	
Exchange rate policy	8.1
Monetary, credit, and interest rate policy	9.1
Fiscal soundness and tax stability	10.4
Acceptable and sustained economic growth	42.6
Tolerable and stable inflation level	16.8
Other	13.1
2. Most important aspects related to your company's global strategy:	
Prospects of the domestic market	51.1
Positioning within the region, in order to export to neighboring countries	33.1
Positioning within the region, in order eventually to enter the U.S. market	4.8
Positioning within a region of abundant and cheap inputs in order to export to developed countries	2.6
Other	8.5
3. Most important trade policy elements:	
Present protection level for the domestic market	13.7
Export subsidies	8.5
Reimbursement of import duties on certain imported inputs (duty "drawbacks")	12.2
Absence of quantitative restrictions on imports	29.9
Policy of low tariff rates	29.5
Existence of free-trade zones	3.3
Other	3.0
4. Most important aspects of foreign investment treatment:	
Clear and stable legal framework	37.5
Tax regulations	15.1
Exchange rate regulations	17.9
Possibility of entering various sectors of economic productivity	7.2
Double-taxation treaty with country of origin of foreign investment	1.4

Absence of nationalization risk	13.7
Intellectual-property laws	4.5
Other	2.7

5. Most important "microeconomic" elements:

Skilled work force	25.0
Competitive salary structure	18.1
Adequate labor laws	18.1
Anticipation of privatizations	3.5
Adequate infrastructure	16.7
Availability of natural resources	4.9
Adequate supply of inputs	11.1
Other	2.8

6. Most important among the foregoing five subject areas:

Macroeconomic policy (question 1)	31.5
Your company's global strategy (question 2)	33.1
Colombian trade policy (question 3)	11.7
FDI treatment (question 4)	13.2
"Microeconomic" elements (question 5)	10.4
Other	0.0

7. Three main reasons that might cause the foreign investor in your company to increase investment in Colombia:

Improvement in the public-order situation	33.3
Greater macroeconomic stability	17.5
Better "microeconomic" conditions (in the sense of question 5 above)	11.6
Better treatment for foreign investment (in the sense of question 4 above)	11.9
Greater trade integration with neighboring countries	14.5
Greater trade integration with the United States	2.6
Ratification of MIGA (on public order) by the Colombian Ccngress	2.6
Other	5.9

Source: FEDESARROLLO.

Table 4.15. FDI Companies and National Companies vis-à-vis the Liberalized Domestic Market: Survey Responses

	National total	By size of company			Exporter total	By Market		
		Large	Medium	Small		High export proportion	Small export proportion	No exports
Describe your company's position vis-à-vis the imported products competing with it in the domestic market.								
a. Excellent (low risk of losing market share)		12.5	12.5	—	10.4	8.3	11.1	16.7
b. Good (moderate risk of losing market share)		66.7	62.5	—	62.5	66.7	61.1	61.1
c. Fair (high risk of losing market share)		20.8	20.0	50.0	22.9	16.7	25.0	16.7
d. Poor (danger of disappearing from market)		—	2.5	50.0	2.1	8.3	0.0	5.6
Number of companies that responded	66	24	40	2	48	12	36	18
Describe your company's position vis-à-vis the imported products competing with it in the domestic market.								
a. Excellent (low risk of losing market share)		14.1	13.4	12.9	12.5	16.3	10.9	14.6
b. Good (moderate risk of losing market share)		69.0	64.9	62.9	64.6	61.3	66.1	65.6
c. Fair (high risk of losing market share)		12.7	16.8	21.6	17.9	15.0	19.1	16.7
d. Poor (danger of disappearing from market)		1.4	2.6	0.9	1.9	3.8	1.1	2.1
Number of companies that responded	455	71	268	116	263	80	183	192

Source: FEDESARROLLO business opinion survey, special section on trade liberalization, March 1994.

rank high in companies' possible approaches to confronting the new competition is to export to the regional market. This holds true for the total as well as for the firms disaggregated sector by sector. Of less importance is production in a country with cheap inputs in order to reexport to developed countries, or the possibility of entering the U.S. market through an eventual Colombian-U.S. free trade agreement.

Among the most important macroeconomic determinants are a "sustained and acceptable economic-growth level" and "tolerable and stable inflation level." This result harmonizes with the importance given the FDI firm's "global" strategy: the presence of multinationals is justified by the dynamics of domestic demand which is closely linked to economic stability in terms of growth and inflation. Such factors as exchange rate policy, fiscal soundness, and monetary and credit policy were not singled out as determinants. Respondents possibly considered these factors to be merely characteristics of sustained and stable growth and not necessarily attractive in themselves. Nevertheless, it is still surprising to discover the small significance attached to that policy considering that the survey was formulated at a time of Colombia's actual engagement in an interesting debate over exchange rate policy.

With respect to the influence of the juridical framework, although it only ranks third, it nonetheless plays a significant role. The surveyed firms emphasized the importance of having clarity and stability. The factors that were judged least important in determining investment were microeconomic factors, among which the only one that seemed especially influential was the presence of a skilled work force (Table 4.14, question 5), considered the most important microeconomic factor in all sectors.[18]

Looking toward the future (Table 4.14, question 7), the greatest obstacle to generating higher levels of investment is the public order situation. More than 33 percent of investors stated that an improvement in this area would lead them to increase their FDI levels.[19] Interestingly, Colombia recently signed a bilateral treaty with England[20] to protect investments from that country against insecurity and violence—thereby seeking to neutralize some of the FDI-inhibiting effects of the public order problem, in order to attract greater levels of investment into the country. This measure reflects very clearly the turnaround in Colombia's attitude toward foreign investment. In their responses regarding factors that might lead them to increase their FDI levels, the firms did not attach much significance

---

[18] This lack of importance attributed to microeconomic factors harmonizes with findings from studies of FDI determinants in other countries. Kravis and Lipsey (1982) found that market size has a positive influence on investment while relative costs of labor play only a marginal role.

[19] Nevertheless, it is curious to note that no responding firm included MIGA among its preferences. This is an insurance against potential damages from the public order situation.

[20] As of this writing, not yet ratified by the Colombian Congress.

to the potential benefits to them of any future Colombian trade integration with the United States. More important to them were the prospects for trade integration with neighboring countries.

The public order question was important to all firms, but other factors within this same category of issues that would affect future investment seemed to vary in importance according to the economic sector of the responding FDI firm. For instance, trade integration with other Latin American countries is of vital importance for firms from certain sectors (petroleum derivatives, chemical products, rubber and plastics), while the same issue is not as crucial for the metalworking sector and is totally without relevance for the nonmetallic minerals sector, for which microeconomic conditions is the second most important factor.

Contribution to Development and Transfer of Technology

Foreign direct investment can produce at least three beneficial effects for the recipient country—namely, inflow of foreign exchange, an increase in the economy's capital stock, and transfer of technology. By technology, we mean "the stock of know-how (technical or managerial) utilized in production and marketing" (UN, 1992). Technological change can contribute to growth via the following three channels: increases in productivity of inputs through innovation in production processes; introduction of new products; or improvements in export performance through a transition toward products with greater technological content.

Transnational enterprises are considered to be the principal conduit of technology transfer (Grossman and Helpman, 1992). According to a 1993 United Nations report, more than four-fifths of U.S. technology transfer income derives from affiliated companies. Furthermore, there is not much question about multinational enterprises' technological superiority. Our survey results seem to confirm this primacy: some 64.7 percent of the responding firms considered their technological assets to be their principal advantage over national firms (Table 4.16, question 1).[21] Foreign enterprises usually operate in industrial branches characterized by high capital intensity; they have better-qualified personnel; and they have higher levels of productivity (Misas, 1993). If the firms answered the question while thinking of comparable local firms, then one could conclude that the multinationals bring in more sophisticated technology than that utilized by local firms.

---

[21] This result accords well with the nucleus of modern theory on FDI. In the tradition of Hymer-Kindleberger (Buckley and Casson, 1989), the existence of transnational firms is explained by a specific advantage on the part of foreign companies, because in order to compete with national firms, who know the domestic market well, the multinationals must have such a compensatory advantage.

In order to evaluate the potential of technology transfer, it would be interesting to see if the branches have potential for technological development and if there occurs a consequent dissemination of this technical know-how toward the national business sector. Our survey tried to evaluate some of these points. Firms were asked if they provided training courses, if they had subcontracts with national producers for the production of intermediate goods, if they developed their own products, and what percentage of their staff was engaged in research and development activities.

The results give a not very optimistic image of the FDI subsidiaries' potential in terms of the desired technological effort and the dissemination of technology toward the domestic sector. Most of the responding firms make additional investments simply to expand production using their existing technology (Table 4.16, question 2), which contributes little to the transfer of new technologies. Only in the nonmetallic minerals sector had recent investments been made to introduce new production techniques. Generally, however, the products involved were of low technological content.

The technology utilized comes in most cases from the parent company, both overall and sectorally. Interestingly, only the nonmetallic products sector has clearly indicated that it develops its own products. These results apparently confirm what other studies have suggested—namely, that branches tend merely to modify and adapt innovations created in the parent company, seldom developing their own products and production processes.

Some 62.3 percent of the surveyed firms, both sectorally and generally, did claim to have adapted some of their products to the Colombian milieu (Table 4.16, question 4). In order to ascertain the potential for technology transfer through product differentiation, the same firms were later asked if these adaptations involved the product's packaging, labeling, consumer information, chemical composition, net weight, product state, or other aspect. The result was that three of the 13 surveyed firms then said that no adaptation had been made, and for seven firms the differentiation consisted only of minor adaptations (change of label, package size, or information provided to the consumer).

Research expenditures (Table 4.14, question 6) are equal to less than 3 percent of sales totals, except for chemical products, petroleum derivatives, rubber and plastics sectors, where companies expend an average of 6 percent. These percentages are rather high, because according to 1992 United Nations figures, 10 enterprises of great importance worldwide expend the equivalent of 2 percent to 6 percent of their sales income on research.

There seems to be a small margin for industrial cooperation between foreign and domestic enterprises: some 40 percent of the firms confirmed that they had no type of subcontracts for the production of intermediate goods (Table 4.16, question 8), while 55 percent did have subcontracts. A secondary survey, carried out to obtain more precise information in this regard, revealed that these subcon-

Table 4.16. Contribution to Development, According to Survey Responses

	Percentage of responses
1. If you believe that your firm is at an advantage vis-à-vis fully nationally owned firms because of your cooperation with foreign partners, please indicate, in order of importance, the three most favorable factors, from among the following list:	
The company has intra-company marketing channels unavailable to national firms	9.1
The company has exclusive technological assets	25.2
It has access to superior technological assistance because of the association with foreign partners	39.5
It has a good name among consumers because of foreign participation	19.2
It has cheaper financing than that available to national firms	4.5
Other factors	2.4
2. If your enterprise has recently (past two years) made additional investments, what was their objective? (If more than one of the following responses would apply, please indicate their order of importance.)	
To expand production using present technology	37.4
To introduce new products	25.8
To modify products already existing in other branches/affiliates or in the parent company	2.1
To modify products that your firm has already been producing	7.4
To introduce new production techniques	27.4
3. What is the source of the technology for your firm's production process? (If more than one of the following sources would apply, please indicate their order of importance.)	
Technology purchase from a third party in the FDI's host country	2.3
Technology purchase from a third party in a developed country	10.3
Parent company	59.3
Own technological creation	12.0
Improvement and adaptation of parent company technology	16.1
4. If your firm has a parent company, are some of the products your firm is selling in Colombia different from the products produced by the parent company?	
Yes	62.3
No	37.3

5. If your answer to the previous question was "yes," where was the modified product developed?

In the firm in Colombia	93.8
In the parent company	6.3

6. If your firm has a research and development department, approximately how large are the expenditures of this department, as a proportion of sales?

3.0

7. What percentage of your firm's staff is engaged in research and development activities?

0% to 10%	97.0
11% to 20%	3.0
More than 20%	0.0

8. What percentage of the total value of your firm's production do your subcontracts amount to? (By "subcontracts," we mean a contract with a given domestic producer from outside your firm to produce some intermediate good for your firm for a predetermined period and in accordance with contract specifications.)

1% to 25%	54.9
26% to 50%	3.9
51% to 75%	0.0
76% to 100%	2.0
No such subcontracts	39.2

9. If your firm does subcontract domestically or regionally, what are the main reasons?

To simplify our firm's operation, producing a reduced number of components	22.4
To reduce costs through specialization	41.4
To avoid stockpiling large inventories of inputs, through timely arrival of inputs	5.2
To take advantage of small and medium-sized suppliers' superior response flexibility	10.3
Existence of affiliates of our firm domestically (or regionally) with the ability to supply the subcontracted inputs	17.2
Other	3.4

10. If your firm exports, how many cents' worth of imports do you bring in per dollar's worth of goods that you export?

349.1

Source: FEDESARROLLO.

tracts in no case exceeded a level of 19 percent of production and that the usual level was more on the order of 2 percent. This percentage is especially low in regard to the subcontracting of domestic production of intermediate goods in the sector producing clay, china, porcelain and glass products. This finding accords with the explanation given by the majority of companies that have subcontracts: the FDI firms' desire first, to reduce their costs through specialization, and second, to simplify their plant operations. The potential for separating production processes appears small, as does the associated potential for specialization in intermediate goods.

Here it would be helpful to differentiate among the three different elements that constitute technology transfer. First, with regard to the transfer from the parent company to the branches, apparently foreign enterprises transfer technology that gives them an advantage vis-à-vis domestic companies. Second, with regard to the transfer of knowledge from the foreign sector to the domestic sector, the results are mixed: there is no real innovation in the multinational enterprises in terms of products or production processes—which is not surprising and occurs also in other developing countries besides Colombia. There does exist a small potential for the transfer of know-how through the adaptation of products, but it is not possible to determine the magnitude of this potential. And third, with regard to the dissemination of technology toward the domestic business sector, little can be expected from subcontracting, and furthermore, it is clear that some sectors have very little potential for expanded subcontracting at some future time. The largest potential for technology transfer resides perhaps in the country's mixed enterprises, which, through close cooperation between the foreign and national partners, can lead to greater dissemination of technologies. In this regard, it is important to note that mixed enterprises clearly cannot be created in all sectors— a limitation that needs to be borne in mind during the design of eventual incentives for the transfer of technology through such enterprises.

Our survey also sought to ascertain foreign firms' contribution to Colombia's trade balance (question 10). Both overall and sectorally, the balance is negative. At the aggregate level, exports represent only 29 percent of imports—a share much lower than the national average (Misas, 1993). Sectorally, the nonmetallic minerals sector is apparently the only one showing a relatively balanced import-export performance. These results are consistent with earlier findings: enterprises with FDI are oriented primarily toward the domestic market. The results suggest also that foreign companies are quite dependent upon imported inputs, and explain their receptivity to import liberalization and their relative lack of concern about exchange rate management during a time of growing pressure toward revaluation.

Conclusion

Colombia has experienced notable progress in its laws on FDI. At present, except for taxes on profit remittance, foreign capital receives the same treatment as that accorded to domestic capital. If we exclude the petroleum and mining sectors (the determinants of which are not usually the same as for other sectors), FDI in Colombia has not been significant in comparison with FDI in many other Latin American countries, although clearly an important FDI increase took place starting in 1993. It is still not certain whether this recent increase reflects a new trend or merely a temporary influx of investments that had been postponed.

Most of the enterprises surveyed are old, large and mainly owned by foreigners. In general, they orient their production toward the domestic market, and when they do export, it is primarily to other Latin American countries. The major foreign investment determinants are fully in keeping with the foregoing. Most of these firms were attracted by the possibility of supplying the domestic market. For that reason, they consider an official economic policy that is conducive to greater and more stable growth as an essential precondition for expanding their investment. These firms display a favorable attitude toward integration with neighboring countries but relative indifference toward any eventual integration with the United States. In addition, they believe themselves to be well positioned to face the challenges inherent in Colombia's economic liberalization.

Although the enterprises based on foreign capital have access to superior technology, thereby giving Colombian consumers access to better products, these enterprises' technology transfer potential is thus far not very apparent. Such companies perform little research, they do not differentiate their products significantly from parent company products, and, most of all, they do very little domestic subcontracting. Like the results of different FDI studies on a wide range of countries, our survey results indicate that, at least thus far, FDI's principal benefits in Colombia will have to be sought in areas other than the transfer of technology.

Bibliography

Agosin, M., J.R. Fuentes, and L. Letelier. 1994. Los capitales extranjeros en las economías latinoamericanas: el caso de Chile. In *Los capitales extranjeros en las economías latinoamericanas,* ed. J.A. Ocampo. Red de Centros de Investigación Económica Aplicada. Bogota: Inter-American Development Bank and FEDESARROLLO.

Banca y Finanzas. 1988. Ponencia para el primer debate del proyecto de ley 80 de 1988. Bogota (October).

_____. 1989. Ponencia para el primer debate del proyecto de ley 242 de 1988. Bogota (October).

Banco de la República. 1992. Transición del régimen cambiario colombiano, notas editoriales. In *Revista del Banco de la República* (June). Bogota.

_____. 1989. *Metodología para la elaboración de la balanza de pagos.* Bogota.

_____. 1987. *Colombia, 20 años del régimen de cambios y de comercio exterior.* Bogota.

Brewer, T. 1991. *Foreign Direct Investment in Developing Countries.* Working Papers (June). World Bank, Washington, D.C.

Buckley, P., and M. Casson. 1989. *The Economic Theory of the Multinational Enterprise.* London: MacMillan.

Buitrago, O. 1991. *Carta de gerencia* 610 (November). Legis Editores, Bogota.

Cock, J. E. 1990. Las regalías variables: un incentivo para la exploración de hidrocarburos. *Estrategia económica y financiera* (No. 147, September). Bogota.

Departamento Nacional de Planeación (DNP). 1993. *Business Guide for Foreign Investment in Colombia.* Bogota.

Echavarría, J. J., and P. Esguerra. 1990. Empresas transnacionales y reestructuración industrial en Colombia. FEDESARROLLO-ECLAC, Bogota. Mimeo.

Economic Commission for Latin America and the Caribbean (ECLAC). 1993. Tendencias recientes de la inversión extranjera directa en América Latina y el Caribe: elementos de políticas y resultados. Santiago, Chile (May). Mimeo.

_____. 1992. *Inversión extranjera en América Latina y el Caribe 1970-1990.* Vol. 2. DSC/1/Add.1 (September). Santiago.

Fanelli, J. M., and M. Damill. 1994. Los capitales extranjeros en las economías latinoamericanas: Argentina. In J.A. Ocampo, ed., *Op. cit.*

FEDESARROLLO. 1994. *Encuesta de opinión empresarial, módulo especial sobre la apertura económica.* Bogota (April).

Garay, L.J., and D. Pizano. 1979. La decisión 24: su impacto en Colombia (un estudio de campo). In *El grupo andino, objetivos, estrategia, mecanismos y avances,* eds. L.J. Garay and D. Pizano. Bogota: Pluma Ed.

García, A. 1992. Bases de la integración financiera entre Colombia, México y Venezuela. *Banca y finanzas* (No. 25, July-September). Bogota.

Grossman, G., and E. Helpman. 1992. *Innovation and Growth in the Global Economy.* Cambridge, Mass.: The MIT Press.

Guisinger, S. 1986. Para atraer y controlar la inversión externa. *Perspectivas Económicas* (No. 57). United States Information Agency, Washington, D.C.

Informe Especial sobre Inversión Extranjera en Colombia. 1984. *Economía Colombiana* (No. 159, July). Bogota.

Koechlin, T. 1992. The determinants of the location of USA direct foreign investment. *International Review of Applied Economics* 6 (2).

Kravis, I. B., and R.E. Lipsey. 1982. Location of Overseas Production for Export by U.S. Multinational Firms. *Journal of International Economics* 12 (3/4), May.

Legislación Económica. 505 (1973): 531 (1974); 544 (1975); 754 (1984); 836 (1987); 872 (1989); 921 (1991); 926 (1991); 939 (1991).

Ministerio de Hacienda. 1993. La inversión extranjera en Colombia y la tributación. Bogota. Mimeo.

Misas, G. 1993. *El papel de las empresas transnacionales en la reestructuración industrial de Colombia: una síntesis.* Estudios e Informes de la CEPAL No. 90. Santiago.

Montenegro, A. 1983. La crisis del sector financiero colombiano. *Ensayos sobre política económica* 4 (Dicembre). Bogota.

Mora, L. 1984. Los nuevos incentivos a la inversión extranjera y la balanza de pagos. *Economía colombiana* 155 (July). Informe especial sobre inversión extranjera en Colombia. Bogota.

Ocampo, J.A., ed. 1994. *Los capitales extranjeros en las economías latino-americanas.* Red de Centros de Investigación Económica Aplicada. Bogota: IDB and FEDESARROLLO.

Ocampo, J.A., and R. Steiner. 1994. Los capitales extranjeros en las economías latinoamericanas. In J.A. Ocampo, ed., *Op. cit.*

Ros, J. 1994. Mercados financieros y flujos de capital en México. In J.A. Ocampo, ed., *Op. cit.*

Schneider, F.S., and B. Frey. 1985. Economic and Political Determinants of Foreign Direct Investment. *World Development* 13 (2).

Tenjo, F. 1992. Vivimos en un paraíso fiscal! *Estrategia económica y financiera* (July). Bogota.

United Nations. 1993. *World Investment Report 1993.* New York.

_____. 1992. *World Investment Report 1992.* New York.

Zuleta, L.A. 1992. Privatización en Colombia: experiencias y perspectivas. Report presented by FEDESARROLLO to the Inter-American Development Bank. Bogota.

Index

Esguerra, P., 161, 163
Exchange rate policy
  Colombia, 138, 143-44
  recommendations for, 33
Export diversification, Chile
  factors influencing policy for, 105
  role of FDI in, 3, 11, 27, 130, 133
Exports
  FDI's role in position of host country, 3
  manufacturing in Latin America for, 10
  Argentina
    auto parts and finished vehicles, 80-82,
      95-96
    FDI's impact on, 27
    food and beverage manufacturers and
      beverage products, 82
    manufacturing sector, 74-78
  Chile
    orientation of FDI toward, 27
    volume levels, 105
  Colombia, 161, 163, 165, 169

Fanelli, J.M., 44, 149n9
FEDESARROLLO, Colombia, 159, 162t, 163t,
  164t, 165, 166-67t, 168t, 172-73t
Ffrench-Davis, R., 11, 14, 21, 27, 106
FIEL (Fundación de Investigaciones Económicas
  Latinoamericanas), 70n34, 87t
Financial sector
  Chile
    external debt instruments sold in, 13-14
    FDI contributions in, 27-28, 123
    FDI inflows to (1987-93), 111f, 113t, 115t,
      116
    liberalization of foreign capital access, 21,
      122-23
  Colombia
    crisis (1980s), 142
    regulations on FDI in, 15
    regulatory reform, 142
    special FDI regulations (1991), 140-43
  See also Banking system; Capital market
Food and beverage manufacturers, Argentina
  levels of FDI (1990-93), 68-69, 74-78, 91
  product quality and productivity, 91

research and development in by export-
  oriented, 94
trade, 75-77, 79, 82
Foreign direct investment (FDI)
  factors in attracting investments, 2
  increase in Latin America, 1, 4-7
  internationalization of markets with, 26-28
  liberalization of policies in Latin America,
    17-18
  prospects in Latin American countries for, 3
  recommended reform of Latin American
    policy for, 30
  Argentina
    determinants and microeconomic impact,
      58-94
    factors in new capital inflows, 18, 39-40
    impact on trade, 27
    liberalized policy for, 8, 11
    redefinition of policies, 98-102
  Chile
    contribution to technology, 131-32
    determinants of recent increases (1987-93),
      120-24
    empirical model for analysis, 120-22
    evolution (1987-93), 110-12
    legal framework regulating, 105-20
    liberalized policy for, 11
    quantitative analysis of behavior, 122
    role in total national investment, 124-27,
      128t
    technological contributions of, 3-4
  Colombia
    defined, 144
    determinants of, 164-70
    liberalized policy for, 11
    sources of (1970-93), 148, 152-53t
    survey, 158-75
    technological contribution of, 3-4
  Mexico, 22
Foreign enterprises. See Transnational enterprises
  (TEs)
Foreign Investment Committee, Chile, 107-8
Foreign Investment Law, Argentina, 44
Foreign ownership participation, Argentina, 42
Frey, B., 158n12
Fuchs, M., 45